Dummy
With
Desire

Dummy
With
Desire

by

Orest Cole

RIVERCROSS PUBLISHING INC.
Orlando

ISBN: 1-58141-027-1

Library of Congress Catalog Card Number: 95-50195

First Printing

Library of Congress Cataloging-in-Publication Data

Cole, Orest, 1918-
    Dummy with desire / by Orest Cole.
        p.   cm.
    ISBN 1-58141-027-1
    1. Cole. Orest, 1918-   . 2. Executives—United States-
-Biography. 3. United States. Navy—Biography. 4. Grocery trade-
-United States. 5. Swift-Eckrich, Inc. 6. Cole, Orest, 1918-
I. Title.
HD9321.95.C65A3   1999
381'.148'092—dc21
    [B]   98-50195
                                                                      CIP

DUMMY WITH DESIRE

I wrote this book for one reason—to try to show that someone with an average intelligence can be reasonably successful in life. In my thinking the two keys are desire and planning.

I would like to thank all the people I have done business with and all Eckrich personnel, especially Mr. Henry Eckrich, now deceased, for hiring me. I think I have rubbed elbows with some of the finest people in the world. They were great to me. I thank Herman Eckrich, deceased, for inviting me back from the service to work for his company. John Norton (deceased) for hiring a person that could hardly drive a car and didn't know how to drive a truck.

Joc Helmkamp (deceased) for saving my job in Brazil Indiana.

Eugene (Bud) Eckrich (deceased) for helping me.

Bud Lill for understanding my problems opening new territories.

Don Menga for teaching an old man new sales techniques.

Most of all my terrific family.

Dummy
With
Desire

CHAPTER 1

My name is Orest Cole. I was born on a farm just outside Leavenworth, Indiana, on October 5, 1918. My parents were Anna Green Cole and Luther Cole. We lived on my grandfather's farm with him and his daughter, Anna, who never married.

Although my father was considered one of the better farmers in the area, we were very poor. My mother always wore a gingham dress, and my father always wore a pair of bib overalls. This was a depressed area. There was no industry. Most people were either farmers or bootleggers. As for religion, people were either deeply religious, or had none at all.

My father was a large man in his day—six feet tall and about 180 pounds. He was a very generous man, who helped people in trouble just because they needed it. Most other people around there did the same.

In those days all young people were expected to work. When I was about eight I hoed corn with a murderer—a fellow named Jess Bird who had a large black birth mark that covered almost half of his face. Jess had murdered a man named Neil Curtis, for making fun of his face. My dad put up his bail and was responsible for him before the trial. I hoed corn with Jess before the trial. We farmed along a creek by the name of Dry Run. There were thick trees along the creek bank and each time there was a gust of wind Jess would stop, jerk out his gun and point it at the trees. He was scared all the time. Being only eight years old, I thought Jess was a coward. In my mind brave man did not fight that way.

After serving only a short time in jail, Jess was paroled but some time later he shot and killed another man and went back to prison.

My father had a brother, Ira, who had a large family of boys and on rare occasions we visited them. The boys liked nothing better than to get me on a swing in the barn and swing me until there was slack in the rope. I was a sickly, skinny kid with asthma and that swinging scared me half to death because I knew I was going to fall out. I'm quite sure being frightened and fragile along with not being accepted by other kids caused my asthma. And in fact five years later after we moved to Antwerp, Ohio, and I was accepted by the kids, my asthma disappeared.

My cousins' greatest sport seemed to be throwing muddy manure-soaked corn cobs at each other. Once I saw one of them with a perfect print of a corn cob on his cheek. Those heavy cobs must have hurt a lot. It's a wonder they didn't get an infection.

In the second grade I was badly cut on the chin. I was sliding down a hill on a sled at the school yard, the sled turned over and I cut my chin on a rusty tin can. It was a jagged wound cut to the bone. The teacher stretched me out across his desk, held the wound open and cleaned it out with iodine. Now, at age eighty, I still have the scar.

Because I was absent from school over thirty days I failed the third grade and was held back. When my classmates found out they teased me unmercifully pointing their fingers at me saying, "You're a dummy. We're glad you won't be in our class next year. We don't like dummies." I carried this hurt for many years.

My mother's cousin, Ike Breeden, was a farmer on an out-of-the-way strip of land near the Ohio River where some people used to make moonshine whiskey. The place was called Potato Run. Ike was going to Detroit to work in a factory, so he was having a farm sale. Dad decided to go so he rented a boat owned by a very religious man known as Uncle Jimmie.

Ike had two sons who were around 13 or 14 years old at the time. His wife belonged to the Briales family who were bitter enemies of the Lowes family. Both families were bootleggers and both families were at the sale. Everyone was surprised because they couldn't understand why the families were suddenly getting along since they had always been such bitter enemies.

At those sales soup was always served. The soup never ran out because people just keep adding water. As the day wore on the soup was known as "water soup."

During lunch someone shot a gun through the kitchen ceiling, and all hell broke loose. To this day I have never seen a fight scene that compared to that even in the movies. Men were fighting with guns, rocks, clubs and fists. No one was killed, but one man who was hit over the head with a fence post was never the same. People were screaming and running in all directions. It was fierce. Mom gathered my sister and me up and, along with Uncle Jimmie, we headed for Uncle Jimmie's boat. We left my father. He could take care of himself. As we approached the river two men stepped out from the bushes and asked Uncle Jimmie what he wanted. Uncle Jimmie replied, "Nothing, brother." They told us to go on. Mother, sister and I were scared, but Uncle Jimmie was as cool as a cucumber.

The only drinking water we had was cistern water. We cleaned the cistern once a year, in the fall when the water line was low. I remember one time we cleaned it out and found a half-decayed rat. We had been drinking the water and the whole time that rat was lying in it.

In the winter we took a bath once a week in a wash tub. Several people used the same water, because we had to save water. In the summer we bathed in the creek, about a mile from the house. Mother and Aunt Ann washed the clothes with home-made lye soap in that same creek.

We had an outside toilet. For toilet paper we used a Sears catalog. When this ran out we used the softest corncobs we could find. Take it from me there were no soft ones.

Most of our food was home-grown. We butchered our meat, smoked and cured our hams and bacon in our smoke house. We cooked and canned the other meat. We canned vegetables and fruit too. Nothing went to waste. About the only things we purchased at the store were seasonings.

Tuberculosis was very prevalent in those days. One day while I was standing on the ground at school under a window, a young lady vomited blood from the second floor just missing me. She died soon after.

My grandparents on my mother's side lived in Leavenworth, which was near the Ohio River. There were often floods in the spring. One time I stepped out of their upstairs window into a boat to go to school. Their home had no foundation. It sat on rocks at each corner. It is a wonder the current didn't take the house down the river. When the water went down, they scraped the mud off the floors and walls and scrubbed them with lye soap. During the floods they moved the furniture upstairs and used what was called a thunder mug—a bucket—for a toilet.

Early in the spring of 1929 my father contracted pneumonia. This was planting time with no one to do the work, so he did not go to bed. He believed he could sweat the poison out by piling on heavy clothes. I could see where he had sweated through all those clothes.

He chewed Star Plug tobacco and smoked Prince Albert tobacco in a corncob pipe, which didn't help his health. He developed lung cancer. He began to spit up blood, then parts of his lungs. He knew he was going to die. He said he wasn't afraid to die, but he sure hated to leave his wife and two small children. He passed away in September. Friends and relatives did the harvesting for mother at no charge. People helped each other in those days.

Really hard times started then. Mother had a sale and put the proceeds in the Leavenworth Bank. The government had just built Dam 44 on the Ohio River. It was completed in early 1929. People were working and had mortgaged their property. Then the market crashed in 1929, everyone was laid off with no way to pay off their mortgaged properties. The bank closed within the week. I believe Mother got about 8% of her money over the next ten years.

My grandfather was old and needed care, and someone had to farm his place. One of his sons moved in to care for him and we all moved into a shack down under the hill—Mother, Aunt Ann (Dad's sister), my sister and I.

This place was almost not liveable. We papered it with old newspapers. I worked for my uncle for 25 cents a week. My aunt helped with grandfather and worked for my uncle's wife for food. Mother went to Ft. Wayne, Indiana, to seek work. After a time she found a job there in a pickle factory.

On his 88th birthday my grandfather fell and broke his hip. In those days surgeons didn't operate on a man of his age, so he just lay in bed until he died. The thing I remember most about Grandfather was his long wavey snow white hair. At 88 he had a full head of hair. I remember seeing him pour whiskey in his hands and put it on his hair each morning. He said this kept his hair growing. Everyone called him Uncle Liman.

Grandfather had an unusual will: if any of his heirs died before he did their children got nothing. So my sister and I got nothing. My family, including Aunt Ann moved to Corydon, Indiana to live with my mother's sister Ila and Joe Lee, her husband. We had to leave our pets behind. Crave Cole kept the cats, Swan Cole took our old dog, Sutt, who was nine years old and had never had a collar on. Swan took the dog to his city home and tied him up. Sutt chewed through the rope and disappeared. Our hearts were broken again. We loved Old Sutt, and he loved us.

Aunt Ila and Uncle Joe Lee had two small children, George and Alice. Uncle Joe had a foreign name and he changed it to Lee. He had fought in World War I and was the most patriotic person I ever knew. He owned a bakery and also sold candy and ice cream. Even though he couldn't read and write very well and had no school smarts he had a head for business. In those days he gave each child a piece of candy when they came into the bakery. It was common knowledge in Corydon that the kids insisted their parents take them to Joe Lee's for bread and candy.

I remember two unusual experiences at Uncle Joe's. He always gave my sister and me candy but one day I decided to get some on my own. He let me know in no uncertain terms that this was off limits unless he gave it to us.

The other time I was, I think, in the fourth grade. I was delivering bread with Uncle Joe in his car house to house. He was driving slowly and I was standing on the fender—cars had fenders in those days—delivering bread to the homes. As he drove past one house, I jumped off the car the wrong way instead of waiting for him to stop and went end-over-end several times. I learned a lesson.

Later when beer became legal Uncle Joe sold the bakery and went into the tavern business. Again he did well and his place became known as the place to come and enjoy a drink. In order to make money he wanted people to come in, have no more than three beers and leave. He believed that people who drank more than that were likely to cause trouble. I heard that if a person started to cause trouble, he would jump over the counter and toss them out.

I sent Uncle Joe my Jap rifle during the World War. He proudly had it displayed at the Corydon V.F.W. If all the people who immigrated this country were as good Americans as Joe Lee we would have a great country.

CHAPTER 2

What a lady my Aunt Ann was! We called her "Maid," like everyone else because she never married. She felt it her duty to help my mother raise my sister and me. To my knowledge, Aunt Ann and Mom never had a harsh word, even after Mom remarried. Nor did I ever hear Mom or Aunt Ann use the Lord's name in vain. Aunt Ann was the nearest thing to a saint that I ever saw or heard about. For her other people always came first. When food was scarce at mealtimes, my sister and I came first even though that usually meant there wasn't much left for her. The only time I ever heard her utter a single bad word was when my brother-in-law, Jake, and I had to go into the service. She said, "Damn, did they have to take them both?"

When my sister married, Aunt Ann lived with her and her husband, Wendell (Jake) Reeb. When their daughter, Kathy, arrived, Aunt Ann helped raise Kathy. Kathy was the third generation of youngsters Aunt Ann helped raise. She had helped raise Dad, being the oldest of eight children and Dad being the youngest. She was devastated when Dad passed on. I remember hearing her say, "Why couldn't it have been me instead of him?" She passed on with throat cancer at the age of 87.

From 1929 through 1932 we attended several schools a year—Leavenworth, Corydon, and three Ft. Wayne schools. The last semester of 1932 we attended Harmar School in Ft. Wayne. I had only one friend, a black boy named J. M. Givens. After the teacher called me a "southern Indiana wash-out" all the white kids shunned me. In those days people from northern Indiana considered people from southern Indiana "hillbillies." J. M.

didn't care what people called me. He was my friend. He had probably been called names, too.

In Ft. Wayne the four of us lived with Mom's sister Meda Klinger, her husband Earl, and her daughter Wadeen and son-in-law, Harvey Nickleson—four families living in five rooms with one bath. Of this group, only mother and Uncle Earl were employed.

We moved to Antwerp, Ohio in the summer of 1933 where Mother's new husband, Joseph Griswold, lived. Trouble seemed to follow us around. Just after moving, the pickle factory where Mom and Joe worked closed. Mom was able to transfer with the company to Grand Rapids, Michigan but Joe was laid off.

Mother had never driven a car before, but she drove from Antwerp to Grand Rapids to work, returning home each weekend. After Joe found work, Mother quit work until World War II was declared. Mother never drove after quitting the pickle factory. The good Lord had to be on her side, because she really could not drive.

I started going to school at Antwerp in the fall of 1933 and I was assigned a seat directly behind Evelyn Seslar. She was so pretty, I knew from day one that I was going to marry her. Money was hard to come by in 1933, yet each day for an entire year I gave her a package of Goldtip gum. I was quite sure that she never thanked me for a single package, but I wasn't discouraged. I knew I was going to marry her. I asked God to let me do this.

Antwerp school was much easier than Indiana. I am sure it was because I was accepted by both my teacher, Mr. Clemmer, and the kids. After all those years my asthma left at once. I was still skinny, but now I could join the kids in play.

Starting in the eighth grade I made my own way—earned money for my clothes and my spending money. The summer of 1934 I dug clams, and my sister and I delivered the evening paper, The News Sentinel, a Ft. Wayne paper. I convinced my sister that the south end would be closer to home than the north end. I wanted the north end because Evelyn's parents were customers. Occasionally I would get to see Evelyn. I sometimes got a chance to play with the boys next door to Evelyn. What a thrill when I saw her!

My sister and I always seemed to be able to find work. During the summer we picked strawberries, then tomatoes and later potatoes. All four of us did this—Mother, Aunt Ann, sister and me. During the early summer when we were picking strawberries we had strawberries for lunch. When we picked tomatoes, we had tomato sandwiches, two slices of bread and sliced tomatoes. We cleaned our hands by mashing tomatoes and rubbing them over our hands like soap. I also topped sugar beets in the fall. This was back breaking, cold, hard work because they were partly frozen.

My Mother was very proud of us. We had seen her and Aunt Ann raise us under terrible conditions. My mother had her life planned until the day she died. Mother planned her time and tasks by the week. She wasted no time. She lived until she was 83. I remember her saying, "I have told the Lord I am ready." She died in her sleep. I have been told many times that I am a tenacious man. This is a trait that I got from my mother, which I appreciate very much.

During my freshman and sophomore years Evelyn and I had the same home room, but other than the times we were in class this and sometimes when I delivered the paper, I seldom saw her. I did buy her candy for Christmas. I would throw it onto her front porch and yell, "Candy for Evelyn." She had a boyfriend.

In 1935 Evelyn and I attended a birthday party where we played "spin the bottle." My spin pointed to Evelyn. What a thrill for me! My first kiss with the girl I had thought about since my first day in Antwerp!

CHAPTER 3

I joined the National Guard in 1934. I was just a kid, but kids were better at close order drill than the older men. No one even dreamed of war in those days. I joined for two reasons—the money and two weeks at summer camp at Camp Perry in Ohio. Henry Donnell was our captain. We drilled one night each week which was good training for a youngster. Henry Donnell helped many of us kids get through high school. Henry knew we were not old enough to join but he wanted us to finish school. Times were very hard in 1934.

In the summer of 1936 the National Guard held the largest peacetime maneuvers ever. All of Kentucky, Ohio, Indiana and part of Michigan participated. We lived in pup tents and slept on the ground. That was hard because it seemed to rain day and night.

The last day of camp, as we were packing, we took time out to play football. I got into a fight with a fellow and broke my hand. That's how I found out fights don't pay. My cast read "To be removed 9/16." While the plaster was still wet I changed the 9 to an 8 because I wanted to play football in the worst way. I still have a knot on my hand where the bones did not set properly because the cast was taken off too soon.

There was a scandal in one of the companies in the 148th Battalion. (A company is made up of 64 enlisted men, in this case mostly high school kids.) The kids from Company B or C went to Louisville, near Ft. Knox, and over 30 of them picked up a venereal disease. I was at Ft. Knox Army Hospital with those boys for about five days while the army took several x-rays to make sure the hand was set properly. I left before the other National Guard fellows did.

The career army men called us "tin soldiers" and gave us kids a hard time. They laughed and said that there is no place in the army for kids. Those regular army fellows trained all the time and were in much better shape than the National Guard. To show us how tough they were they would hit each other in their stomachs with their fists.

These years, 1936 and 1937, were two of the best and happiest years of my life. In 1936 I went to work for Carr's IGA stores. I worked after school and on Saturday. To this day I remember my first customer, a Mrs. Smuck. She worked for the Antwerp High School Superintendent. Our adding machine was crude. You punched in the price of each item, and then pulled down a long handle.

I went to work on Saturday at 7:00 a.m. Farmers visited until midnight, then did their shopping. The customer named the item they wanted and the clerk pulled it off the shelf. Waiting on a customer took lots of time.

Joe Carr was the owner. He never criticized the clerks, he just cleared his throat three times. The other clerks had told me this was how he let you know when you were doing something he didn't like.

We had lots of fun during the summer of 1936 having chicken fries and watermelon feasts. We stole them both. Unless the owner got mad, which was rare, we invited him to the party. They always knew who was sponsoring the feast when they were invited.

The fall of 1936 we had a new football coach, Mr. Horney. He was tougher than Mr. Bell, our school principal. Mr. Horney worked us very hard. We were out of condition. We should have been a good team, but we were not. Some of the boys chewed tobacco and spit on the opponent. Some of us put money into a pot and the person who knocked out the opposing star collected the money. We kicked, clawed, or did whatever we thought would get results.

Our uniforms left something to be desired. Our helmets were just a piece of leather. Those who could afford a sponge, put one in the helmet. Some played without kidney and knee pads.

I remember two games in particular. One we played on a baseball field after a heavy rain. The infield was covered with water that came up over our high top shoes. In those days we played both offense and defense. Toward the end of the game I was exhausted mostly because of my soaked uniform. Rex Billman, a spectator, took me to the locker room and gave me two big slugs of whiskey. I went right back to the game.

The other game was a night game at Paulding, our first and last night game. Paulding had two small backs. I knew one, Bun Brown. We were both in the Guards. It was rare for these farm towns to have small people on their team. Our team had only two small people—Wayne Fleck, the quarterback, and me. I played right end. I was six feet tall, but very thin.

I was really keyed up. I thought, wait til I hit this small cuss, he'll be a basket case. The ball went to the other back. Bun hit me low and very hard. I felt as if I would never come down. This was the only time that happened to me. I learned a lesson.

I was never good at offense, but I felt that I could play with the best on defense. One teacher, Mr. Carter, once said to me, ''Why don't you quit horsing around and put on a little weight? You could play on any college team in the country.''

My best friend was Joe Mattingly. He is now dead, but until he became ill he was the toughest young man I had ever met. In practice the first and second teams were divided up. Joe was pitted against me. He enjoyed beating me up. In school no one tried to fight me. They knew they would have Joe to contend with. I have seen him in fights when it seemed that Joe was losing, but when he got in a blow his opponent didn't get up.

In our senior year we went into a new high school building. It was very different from the old building. Each room had a fire alarm, a metal pipe with a bell which ran from the top floor to the bottom floor. One day Joe said, "I'm going to see how that works." Then he rang the bell and pushed me so that I banged into the wall. Since we had the worst reputation of all the students, we were in Mr. Deemer's office almost at once. Mr. Deemer was the Superintendent. He was always strict, and now he was very angry. He said, "I know one of you boys did this. Which one was it? People could have been injured!"

We had just finished gym class and had on tennis shoes. Joe said, "I did it." I said, "Yes, but I pushed him. My shoe was untied. I stepped on the string and pushed Joe. As he was falling, he pulled the bell on the pipe." Mr. Deemer, thank goodness, bought the story. My classmates did not. Many years later at our 50th reunion banquet, I told the story. One man spoke up, "That was not a funny trick, and you didn't kid us."

I was elected Class President my senior year. I felt that I was not qualified and did not deserve this honor because I did not study. I knew I was not going to go to college. I knew I could not do a good job of speaking in front of the class as the Class President was required to do. We also started a newspaper, and I was elected Sales Manager. I could understand this, since I had delivered newspapers for years. Joe and I, like several others, did not attend class regularly. For example, we lined the football field on Friday morning, and played football on Friday afternoon. I missed 24 days of school my senior year. Being the Class President and Sales Manager took some time, but I milked these jobs for all the time possible.

The new school also had a basketball court. I was lucky to make the team as a senior. I recall one time a player went around me with ease. Instinctively I tackled him from the rear. The game was at home and no one knew the rules, so I wasn't thrown off the court.

The coach played three seniors and two sophomores. I asked one of the sophomore players years later why the coach played three seniors. Jack Yeager, who became a dentist, said, "Coach plays the five best athletes." This was good for my ego. Jack was on our football team and went on to become a Little All-American. When he was a senior at Antwerp Jack's team was the only unbeaten unscored on team in its bracket in the state of Ohio. We could have been a good team, if we had listened to the coach, quit tobacco and trained. There are no free rides, as I also found later in life.

On one occasion Joe, Lloyd Young and I took a kid to Ft. Wayne. We hitchhiked. This youngster had never seen a city, street car, or the like. We showed him the town, including the red light district. We did it for kicks and because we wanted to see how he would react. The three of us felt like we were old pros. It is possible that this "educational" trip helped this young man who now owns his own business in Florida. When he made the trip to Ohio for our 50th reunion celebration, he said his father did not appreciate us taking him to Ft. Wayne.

All through high school I had watched Evelyn Seslar mature. I am quite sure that all through the four years I never said a word to her other than an occasional hello. Just before the senior prom she and her boyfriend broke up. I took immediate action and asked her for a date. When she answered "yes," it was the happiest moment of my life. After the prom, we went to see "Pennies from Heaven" with Bing Crosby. We dated every evening after the first date until I had to leave for Guard training at Camp Perry, Ohio.

When Evelyn and her aunt and uncle came to see her cousin Max Seslar and me, I was embarrassed. I was on K.P. and only saw her as she came through the chow line. Willis Friend and I had had a few beers Saturday evening and gotten a little rowdy. After we broke a few bunks we were put on K.P., the price we had to pay for destroying government property.

Max Seslar stayed in the National Guards and became a Major. He was killed in the Pacific during the war. He had corresponded during the war and it was a sad day when my letter was returned to me with the word "deceased" stamped on it.

CHAPTER 4

I knew I had no money to to to college. I was from the poor, very poor side of the tracks. I also knew I didn't need a college degree for a factory job. So after summer camp with the Guards, I went job hunting in Ft. Wayne. Ft. Wayne was about 30 miles from Antwerp, but with no vehicle I had no way home except on weekends. I stayed in Ft. Wayne with a cousin and went home on weekends. Evelyn and I dated each time I was was home.

I applied for a job at every factory in Ft. Wayne with no luck. My Aunt Meda said, ''I used to clean house for Peter Eckrich. I will call his company for you.'' She called and talked with Henry Eckrich, Peter's son. He said, ''Send him over. I'll talk to him.'' He hired me.

Peter Eckrich came to Ft. Wayne from Germany and started a small meat market in his home. Like many people from Germany, he knew how to make sausage products. He expanded the sausage products into a variety of luncheon meats. When I started working for Peter on July 29, 1939 in a new plant he had built on Osage Street in Ft. Wayne.

My first day I reported for work at 4:00 a.m. At 9:00 a.m. we had a coffee break. I felt as though I had already worked my eight hours. I was assigned to the dried beef and bacon crew, packaging these products in a cooler on a concrete floor. I knew then that I did not want to spend the rest of my life doing this. At times the temperature in the bacon cooler was well below zero. My first day I worked from 4:00 a.m. to 8:00 p.m. This was the summer, when there was a big demand for luncheon meats.

25

Eckrich Company was a good place to work but then you were lucky to have any kind of job in those days. In those days the meat industry was a low paying, sloppy, wet place to work. Peter Eckrich and Oscar Meyer are the two companies, in my thinking, that were the foundation of the meat industry in this country. But I always thought Eckrich was the best. The sausage room was as clean as a kitchen in the home, all stainless steel. I started working at 56 cents an hour, with no overtime pay. Al Dirig was my boss. He went on to be manager of a new plant in Fremont, Ohio, some years later. The Erkrich Company had a policy of promoting from within and not laying people off. The lunch meat business in those days died after Labor Day so I was put to work loading sales trucks at night. John Roy was my boss. He was an elderly man, fine and easy going. I was just a kid, and he was almost like a father to me.

I never gave Evelyn a chance to meet anyone else. I married the pretty lady. Her folks had one of the nicer homes in Antwerp. We moved into a furnished apartment at Ft. Wayne. I was working nights. I am sure this was a big let-down, but she didn't complain. We had no vehicle and she was alone at night.

In the spring I transferred back to working days in the sausage room. I was glad to get out of the cooler. I had a sore throat the whole time I worked there. Of course, I was a heavy smoker, which didn't help my throat at all.

I started as a tank washer in the sausage room. This was one of the lowest jobs because I was one of the newest employees. Nick Nausbaum was Plant Superintendent and a fine man.

At that time the companies had sausage makers who made the seasoning for each product. This was the highest paid person in the plant. The man who held the job then was Leo "Pappy" Arend. All the men had come up through the ranks, and the plant was just like a family. Even though Peter Eckrich was retired, he visited the plant frequently. He was proud of his accomplishments. He often said, "If I hadn't made it in the meat business, I would have been a success in the beer business. I was going to work for myself whatever I did.'' I learned a lot from each successful person I worked under. Each one had a special way of managing people.

I knew I did not want to spend the rest of my life making bologna, and I started to plan for the future. We, as a family, had upgraded ourselves. We now lived in a home on Eby Avenue, the same home my aunt used to live in when my Mother moved her family to Ft. Wayne. We were now the proud parents of a daughter, Marilyn Jo. She was prettiest new baby I had ever seen—a blond, blue-eyed girl, with hair in ringlets.

We still did not have a vehicle. I walked to work, about a mile and a half each way. Norm Shaw, a salesman for Eckrich, lived nearby and whenever our paths crossed he picked me up. He sure lived better than I did. He had a new vehicle and a better home.

I took a correspondence course in salesmanship. Since I had worked in a grocery store and as a paperboy there was personal contact with each customer this course was not difficult for me. At that time they guaranteed each graduate a job. I had had good training in most of the aspects of the lunchmeat business and I wanted to remain with Eckrich as a salesman.

Soon we were the parents of another pretty daughter, Judith Kay, with dark hair and blue eyes. I wanted our children to have common names. My name is Orest Gilmore, and no one can pronounce or remember it. I have been called a lot of different names.

I hadn't finished the salesmanship course, but one Saturday morning, the District Sales Manager, John Norton called the house and wanted to speak with me. He told Evelyn he would be at the plant until noon. It was about 11:00 a.m. when he called. In those days we worked six days a week in sales. I was downtown watching a friend, Alex Katas, play tournament pool. Evelyn located me there. I had no vehicle and didn't feel I could risk a cab, so I ran to the plant, about a mile and a half. John said, ''How did you get here so fast, and why are you out of breath?'' I said, ''I ran.'' I got the job as a salesman.

Since I had never had a car and couldn't drive, my step-father gave me a crash course. I also studied for the driving test. The Eckrich salesman's driving records were very important to the company. Harold "Hack" Mosel broke me in as a salesman, but he would not allow me to drive. He was afraid I would spoil his safety record. Hack was a good teacher, but I did not become a good meat salesman in two weeks.

I had never driven a truck, and I was the first salesman at the Branch to learn where the gears were. My first day alone I banged the truck against the wall of the garage several times so I could find out where each gear was before I left the plant.

For refrigeration in those days we had two cream cans in the back of the truck filled with cracked ice and lots of salt. One of the reasons people liked Eckrich products was that it was made of good meat and held up longer in the dinner pail. On the country runs we would be out 10 or 12 hours, and the cracked ice would be completely melted.

We worked six days a week. The customers' refrigeration was not good either in those days. The smaller stores just had ice boxes with blocks of ice to cool the contents. I remember one customer on E. Lewis Street, Mrs. Williams. She must have been around 70 years old, and was less than five feet tall. I called on her store twice a day. She might possibly only buy a half loaf and a ring of bologna.

It was a different world then. We never locked our truck doors.

When I got this sales job, I was very proud. I was only 21 years old. Just old enough to get my truck driver license. I thought I was set for life—good job with an excellent company. I was mistaken. Along came December 7, 1941.

I remember that day clearly. I was listening to the Chicago Bears football game on the radio, when the news of war was broadcast. My family was visiting relatives in Antwerp, Ohio.

Meat became scarce. The company had always purchased meat, mostly fresh pork picnics, on the open market, and now there was none to buy. We started selling salads and baked beans.

Eckrich cut our routes in half. Being the newest salesman, I was the first to go.

I got a job on the railroad as a brakeman. I didn't like it. My run was from Ft. Wayne, west of Chicago; Ft. Wayne to Mansfield, Ohio, east. I didn't like the brakeman job as I was the second man and sat up in what was called the "dog house," a small enclosed area just behind the engine. My job was to sit and watch for "hot boxes" wheels on the train that had become over-heated. This was a very boring job. When I said I was going to quit, I was told, "You can't quit because this is considered a defense job. If you quit we will see that the military service gets you." Cocky me said "That's your privilege." After I left I got a job at Studebaker in Ft. Wayne. They were making airplane parts at the time and made small parts for airplanes. I had never worked with tools, so this was a difficult job.

Here I am on boot leave with my wife and two daughters. I carried this picture throughout the war.

CHAPTER 5

On December 23, 1943, I got a special greeting from the President of the United States. "You have been selected for military duty." I was to report at the bus station in Ft. Wayne on January 3rd and go to Indianapolis for a physical. Out of the bus load, seven were classified 4F, and one was a conscientious objector.

I had heard that the men in best physical condition went into the Navy, but since I had had National Guard training, the fellow who interviewed me said, "You are made for the Marines." I did not want the Marines, so I did the best selling job of my life and was assigned to the Navy. From her my life took a big turn for the worse.

Since I had had Guard training I was put in charge of the company at Great Lakes. Unfortunately the Navy Petty Officer didn't like the way I drilled the fellows, so he took away my special privileges and I was no longer in charge of anything.

We got one leave in boot camp, but we all expected to get another before we left for school to train for a rating. One of my Eckrich customers who had been through the training, had received a rating, and was assigning men to their schools. He told me he would do his best to get me a leave.

When he did not call my name for a school, I asked, "Where do I go?" He said, "You go to sea. You did not pass a test." I found out later that I had only passed one course, Office Work, but I couldn't type so that was out. That was the worst day of my life. I was leaving my wife and two small children and would not see them for . . . how long?

31

They loaded us onto a train in what the Navy called "cattle cars; It was cold as hell.

We were stationed at Camp Shoemaker, California, near Modesto, about 60 miles from San Francisco. It was March, the rainy season. We slept in plywood barracks. You could wring water out of your blanket when you got out of bed. I was miserable with a cold. While at Camp Shoemaker, I had a weekend pass to San Francisco, where I saw sights I had never seen before including men they called homosexuals approaching service men for what they called favors. In the small town I came from you never heard such a word.

Also at Shoemaker, I ran into so-called "misfits," people who had faked insanity or who had shot themselves to get out of battle. They spend the day bragging about escaping the war.

At that time I didn't know what fighting and dying was all about. I was so green I didn't know what to think.

We were taken to Treasure Island, the Navy Embarkation Center. We were told what percentage of us would be casualties and were told about malaria; what a dreadful disease it was, and how we must always sleep under a mosquito net.

We shipped out in what had been a luxury liner, and was now a troop ship. There were five decks of men. I was on the fourth. We were stacked to the ceiling. We had to slide sideways into our bunk. It took a month to get to Milney Bay, New Guinea.

There were Japanese submarines in the water and our ship was blacked out. One time our air conditioner went out when the ship was blacked out. We thought we were going to die. A Marine stood at the top of the ladder with a machine gun, yelling, "The first s.o.b. that steps on that ladder is a dead man!" Several men on the deck below did die during the passage. They were buried at sea. There were so many of us they fed us around the clock.

When we dropped the anchor in Milney Bay, New Guinea, it was night. I saw lights on the shore line, and thought, This can't be so bad. They have electricity. What a rude awakening I had when we hit land.

It rained most of the time and since we slept on the ground under a pup tent it was like sleeping in a sea of mud. There were no mosquito nets. There were mess kits, but no silverware. We whittled forks and spoons out of coconut hulls and used our teeth and hands in place of knives.

There were both pygmies and normal size natives. The pygmies came to about my waist, but they were very strong. The other natives had filed their teeth and wore large rings in their noses and ears. The women had bare, sagging breasts. We were told that they nursed pigs. This was not an unusual sight, it was just part of their culture.

The only English words I ever heard the natives speak were "Smoke, Joe?" They would do almost anything for cigarettes. I was assigned to a detail cutting down virgin timber. After being on the transport, doing nothing for a long period of time, I was really out of shape. We were ordered to cut down so many trees a day and since cigarettes were very cheap, five cents a pack, I gave the pygmies cigarettes to do my work. I was there about two weeks.

My ship was an LCI (Landing Craft Infantry). A dinghy boat from the LCI picked me up and we proceeded to LCI 447. The Captain met me as I came aboard. I did not salute. He coolly shook my hand. He was transferred back to the states soon after that. We had two other officers, Lt. (jg) Bill Sclosser and Lt. (jg) Tagenhorst. We called him Mr. Tag. Mr. Tag told me not to worry about not getting to go to school for a rate. He said, "Don't not feel bad. I will help you get one. Some people get rates faster by experience." He then asked, "May I suggest Quartermaster is the rate you should strike for. Bill, our Quartermaster, is going home soon. I got a rate soon after that, thanks to Mr. Tag. Bill the Quartermaster and Vetter, a Signalman. Vetter sent me semaphores by the hour.

We landed troops on the northern part of New Guinea. We saw little fire, but I am sure the soldiers we landed saw plenty of action when they got inland.

We got a new skipper, S. W. Goldsmith, Jr., a fine man and I found out later, a very brave man. He was also a minister. He had Church each Sunday, but did not force anyone to attend. We spent a lot of time training by going up and down the rivers in New Guinea. The native villages were right along the waters edge, and it was interesting to see how these people lived.

My first sight of death was at Humbolt Bay, New Guinea. A bunch of us were swimming near a number of small boats with their motors running. One fellow got too close and was sucked into the screws of one of the boats. All that surfaced was his guts. I am certain someone went down for the body but I didn't see anyone assigned to do this.

By this time this sort of thing didn't bother me as much as it would have in civilian life. After Navy personnel tells you about casualties that are going to happen, you expect to see death. You do see horrible things but you can't dwell on them.

CHAPTER 6

After New Guinea was secured, we picked up soldiers in New Guinea and proceeded to a small island called Noemfoor. We had the soldiers aboard about twenty-four hours. They were the bravest beat-up group I ever laid eyes on. They had been at Pearl Harbor when war broke out and had fought all the way. They didn't expect to get home and wanted to be there for the invasion of Tokyo if they were alive. These fellows had three and four strings of gold Jap teeth around their necks. They had seen the Japs torture our fellows, they hated them. They said they never took prisoners. Instead they let them surrender, slit their mouths ear to ear, castrated them, shoved their testicles down their throats and then shot them.

These same fellows stood at the fantail, the end of the ship and begged for our scraps as we threw them overboard. They were very thin. Some had frames large enough to carry 180 to 220 pounds, but were down to 135 to 145 pounds with jungle rot all over them. They say Marines are the toughest. We had marines aboard; I say these infantry men were.

If remember correctly they were the 24th division. The American soldier stands head and shoulders over any other fighting man I saw. I believe it is because we have more to live for.

Noemfoor was my first landing where there was heavy enemy fire. Water splashed all around us where shells were landing. Being a quartermaster meant sitting in the pilot house with another person and Elmer, our mascot, a little cur dog. One thing for sure, when General Quarters was sounded I was always the second one in the pilot house—Elmer was first.

When Mr. Tag was ready to lower the ramp after we hit the beach these brave men were standing on deck leaning on their rifles, smoking cigarettes. They looked as calm as you and me going to work on Monday morning. When they hit the beach there was no place to hide even if they had wanted to so, they hit it running. I knew right then I was lucky to be in the Navy.

After we made this invasion we heard rumors that a big one was coming soon. We returned to Humbolt Bay at Hollandia, New Guinea. We rested, chipped paint, and played a little touch football.

We were a flag ship, Group 21 flot 7. Our Lt. Commander, Mr. Ripley, was a career man. His family had been in the armed services since the British days.

Being a Quartermaster, I had access to the ship's logs. When I left for home I took the old log with me. Starting September 23, 1944, through April 28, 1945 I have a day by day account of the L.C.I. 447 activities. What a fine group of people we had aboard. I can't remember hearing an argument among crew members while aboard, but I am sure we had a few since I attended a few Captain Masts. Captain Masts is Navy Court Martial, held when a crew member violated Navy rules. An example would be sleeping on guard duty. It was one of the duties of the Quartermaster to attend and keep records.

I won't mention what we did each day but will do my best to mention the highlights. Beginning September 23, 1944, we started having GQ and fire drills frequently. Elmer must have sensed problems ahead as he started to run to the pilot house each time GQ sounded. Rumors increased daily. On September 27 we took on large amounts of supplies and again on the 29th on October 6, a day after my birthday party.

On October 11 we tied up alongside Liberty Ship John Cabot for rockets. We knew then we would not be carrying troops. Excitement began to build aboard ship. Even though we knew we would be scared no one wanted to be left behind. The sooner the war was over the sooner we would all go home.

It was an all-out war. People saved every way they could, including by buying these War Stamps.

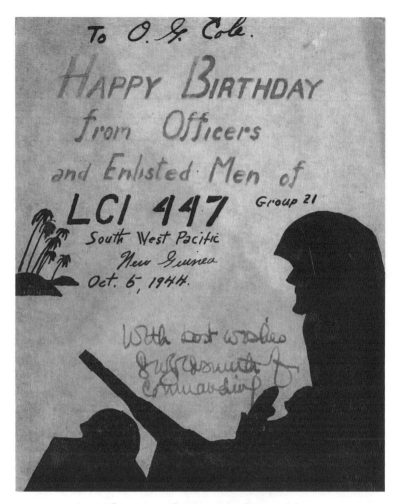

A terrific group of men made this card for me on my birthday in 1944.

On October 12 we were underway. We had rockets, smoke bombs and oil aboard. We started practicing laying smoke screens and taking battle stations. Each day more and more ships joined our convoy. By the end of our journey we had over 1,000 ships of all kinds and sizes. I had never seen a battle wagon, (battle ship), before and it's for sure you can't tell its real size by looking at a picture.

On October 18 we slowed to a crawl. We had a lot of drills which were frightening. We knew the Phillipines were very near. On October 20, "A" day, at 0601 we were at battle stations and stayed there until 1858 when we moored alongside sister ship LCI, 28.

October 21 G.Q., 0604 hours, the Japs wait for no one. All hell breaks loose.

Unless you have actually been in an invasion of this magnitude, you can't imagine how much fire power this many ships can put in the air. It was frightening, rocket ships were firing all rockets on one side of the ship at the same time, producing a solid wall of flaming fire. Men were climbing down rope ladders from the large ships into smaller landing boats going ashore to fight. My heart went out for them. I knew many would be wounded and die.

For the first time we had no troops aboard. We were laying off shore watching all the action. I have never enjoyed seeing the fire works on the fourth of July after seeing this. Nothing I have ever seen compares to the sight of more than 1,000 ships firing at the same time.

We left New Guinea carrying drums of fog oil. Our job was to smoke the air strip at Tacloban. We lay down smoke while anchored very close to the beach.

On October 22, we fired at Jap planes for the first time. We started firing at 6:15 and ceased firing at 6:16.

During calm spells we listened to music and then Tokyo Rose. She would say such things as "Yankee you are going to die." "Your wife is seeing another man!" "Our planes will bomb you at 1200. They will come in from the West.'' And they would. At tree top level so radar could not pick them up.

We were blacked out just off the beach of the airstrip in Tacloban. We knew the Japs could hit us as well as the airstrip, and this was quite frightening. It's hard to describe or visualize what a huge amount of fire power was in the bay.

I have never heard a sound as loud as a rocket ship firing. They would turn broadside and fire the entire salvo on that side, throwing a solid blanket of fire. Our airplane pilots flew above this, firing all the time at the Jap planes. One Jap pilot bailed out and our pilot followed him all the way down firing. Cruel? Yes, but war is kill or be killed.

If I had to pick two groups that I thought were the bravest I would pick the pilots and the group of army infantry we had taken on Noemfoor. The pilots I talked to later at Clark Field were mostly small and very cocky. Also smart. They were getting whiskey from Australia and selling it to us for $50.00 a fifth.

We began hearing rumors the Jap fleet had split and that part of it was coming down through the San Bernardino Strait. Our fighting force was out looking but the north end of the Strait was not protected. So we were sent up through the Strait to delay the Jap force. Were we scared? Hell, yes. Our LCI with 50 mm machine guns was no match for a Jap battleship. Luckily for us the Jap force turned around and headed back out before they got to us. If they hadn't turned around I probably wouldn't be writing this.

October 24th.

We fired many times at the Jap planes. We were also picking up the wounded from ships and taking them to hospital ships. These were long action days.

When anchored we took our regular watches. On a small ship such as an LCI, the Quartermaster stood signal watch, taking his turn with the signalman.

October 25th.
I was on signal watch. The Jap planes came over and engaged in dogfights with our pilots. For a few seconds I just watched and enjoyed the fight. Then I saw a Kamikaze plane aim for a cargo ship on our starboard. It just missed our bow and blew up on impact.

October 27
Some 30 P38's landed at Tacloban. The entire bay became alive with people yelling and waving their arms. It was a very happy time.

October 28
A bomb hit nearby and blew me out of the sack. I was so tired I just got back in bed.

October 29
We were in the middle of a severe tropical storm. These typhoons last about 24 hours—12 hours to reach the peak and 12 hours to recede.

It was very frightening. I had been scared many times but nothing like this. I was scared for two reasons: (1) The storm was fierce and (2) I could tell the bravest man I ever knew was scared. The Skipper asked the Commander: "Shall I send someone below to see that everyone has their life jacket on? I don't think we are going to make it." The Commander said, "No, don't frighten them anymore than they are now. If we go down a life jacket will not save anyone."

The ship was bobbing about like a cork in a bath tub. You couldn't hold the ship within 180 degrees and we were taking a little water in the portholes.

I stayed on the helm many hours. The Skipper felt I had done a good job and I got a commendation. It was the only one he gave out.

We lost some ships. Some as large as the destroyers we called "tin cans." This was wartime, so we did not get the exact number.

November 9th

We had a work detail at Tacloban. Call girls were there for the soldiers and men lined up for at least two blocks. Rumor had it that each man was allowed three minutes.

November 11

We moored starboard of the Indus for beer, the first in ages. We brought 144 cases aboard. The next day other LCIs moored alongside and got their beer rations from us.

November 12

Two Jap planes crashed into the Achilles Liberty ship. Five more ships were hit by Kamikaze planes. What a sad sight, seeing men die. Clarke claimed his first hit, a Jap Zero. Later our gunners shot down a Jap bomber. We called a Jap Betty. We were proud of those two planes on display on our ship's bow.

That day I saw five more ships hit by the Kamikaze pilots. It was a high honor for those pilots to die.

November 14

We landed at Homonhon Island near Leyete Gulf. Part of our group landed troops at Suluan Island nearby. I don't recall any immediate firing from the soldiers, but I know they were as frightened as we were. The longer you survive under these conditions the more scared you became. You see a number of ships hit by Kamikaze planes. You see a number of your sister LCIs hit. You go alongside ammo ships that were hit and the ammo was still exploding, yet the skipper's voice never cracks. Everyone is frightened. If properly trained I think some perform even better. But cowards seem to go completely to pieces; they shake, they vomit, and they can't seem to do anything right.

One day I saw one of our men on deck on his knees, hands clasped. "What are you doing, Clarke?" I asked.

"Praying for the Japs to fly over. I'm from Minnesota and have done lots of hunting but shooting at these Japs is much more fun." He was one in a million.

These men were the crew of LCI 447. Tucker is holding Elmer, our mascot.

December 1

We moored starboard side to U.S.S. Stag, and received the bodies of 100 dead Americans. The Navy does not bury at sea unless it is an absolute must. Most die from burns in the Navy, so the bodies were partly decayed when we received them. We had the bodies aboard lying on a hot metal deck for about 24 hours. We hardly had room to walk. I recall one of the crew handling an arm that had been blown off. It was so decayed it just squirted out of his hands. He took off like he had been shot out of a cannon. It was a very sad day for us.

Christmas Day 1944

This sure as hell was not home. We had church services as did every Sunday led by the Skipper, who was a minister. He did not force us to attend. Our cook, Whiskey Joe, prepared Christmas dinner: half-spoiled mutton Australian style and our usual raisin bread (Bugs were called raisins.).

We got our flour in 50 to 100 lb cloth bags. The bags had weavels from 1 to 3 inches thick on the bags. The sifters could not sift all the weavels out, so we ate them and called them raisins. We also had some fresh cabbage, the first fresh vegetable we had had in months.

THE TALE OF AN LCI

YOU'VE HEARD OF THE CANS AND THE APD'S
AND YOU'VE HEARD OF THE CRUISERS TOO,
AND YOU'VE HEARD OF THE FAST PT'S
AND SOME OF THE THINGS THEY DO.
BUT BROTHER IF YOU'VE A MINUTE TO SPARE
AND FEEL IN THE NEED OF A CRY,
SIT RIGHT DOWN AND MY TALE I'LL SHARE
OF THE TERRIBLE LCI.
THEY'RE A HELLUVA, HORRIBLE LOOKING MESS
NEITHER SHIP NOR BARGE 'TIS TRUE,
THEY'RE A JOKE TO THE FLEET I MUST CONFESS,
BUT NOT TO THE POOR DAMNED CREW.
SHE'LL ROCK AND ROLL ON THE CALMEST DAY
AND SHE'LL BUCK LIKE A KANGAROO,

AND PITCH IN THE MOST PECULIAR WAY,
THOUGH ALL IS SERENE ON THE BLUE.
THE ENGINEERS SIT DOWN IN THEIR HOLE,
THEY CAN'T EVEN HEAR OR THINK.
AND THE BOYS TOPSIDE, AS THEY SWAY WITH THE ROLL,
HAVE OFTEN WISHED SHE WOULD SINK.

THE SIGNALMAN CLINGS TO HIS LIGHT OF THE CON
WHILE SHE HEELS OVER FIFTY DEGREES,
THE HELMSMAN STRUGGLING TO HOLD HER ON COURSE
THOUGH IT'S BLOWING A VERY LIGHT BREEZE.
THE COOKS IN THE GALLEY SOB AND MOAN
AS OVER THE STOVE SLOPS THE STEW,
THEN THE CREW SETS UP A TERRIBLE MOAN,
AND SO BY GOD WOULD YOU.
FOR THE NAVY DON'T CARE IF WE NEVER GET FED,
THEY DON'T EVEN KNOW THAT WE'RE HERE,
SO YOU CAN'T BLAME US BROTHER FOR SEEING RED
WHEN THE REST OF THE GUYS GET BEER.

THE ARMY HELPS OUT WITH ITS CANNED RATION ''D''
BUT NOBODY ELSE GIVES A DAMN,
IT'S A HELLUVA LIFE, I'M SURE YOU'LL AGREE,
WE'RE PRETTY FED UP WITH SPAM.
AND WHEN WE TAKE THE TROOPS ABOARD
TO LAND ON SOME ENEMY SHORE,
THEY TAKE OUR LOOT AND PRAY TO THE LORD
THAT THEY'LL NEVER SEE US ANYMORE.

THEY WERE BUILT, I AM TOLD, OF SOME RUSTY OLD JUNK,
AND STUCK TOGETHER WITH GLUE.
THE WHOLE THING WAS PLANNED BY A HUMOROUS
    DRUNK,
AND AN INMATE OF BUG HOUSE TWO.
BUT DON'T PITY THE FRIEND AND DRY THAT TEAR,
THOUGH WE'RE THANKFUL TO YOU FOR YOUR GRIEF,
WE HAVE SAILED IN THESE THINGS FOR NEARLY A YEAR,
SO SEND US OUR DAMNED RELIEF!!!!!!!!!!!!!!!

January 31

We were at Luzon. Japan is getting closer. Tokyo Rose's broadcasts become less frequent. We knew something big was coming up. We were scared but we wanted to be involved. We knew Japan had to be whipped before we could return home. The longer we were involved in fighting, seeing the dying and wounded, the more frayed our nerves got. We had been very fortunate because we were straffed only once by Jap planes and no one was injured. One person on our crew had a nervous breakdown. I'm quite sure he was an atheist. I think you had better believe in the man upstairs. When I left for the war my neighbors who were Catholic gave me a St. Christopher medal. When things got tough, I must have rubbed that medal a couple dozen times a day.

We had a fine crew. The officers S. W. Goldsmith, Jr., Skipper, T. C. Tagenhorst, W. B. Schlosser, A. J. McCormick and J. D. McDade had a lot to do with this. The Skipper was fair but strict.

It's amazing how people react under battle conditions. All of us were scared, but since we were well-trained and under good leadership we all performed well. Only a few would be so nervous they would throw up. Others who could recognize Jap planes in less than a second on film couldn't recognize them in a number of seconds when the planes were coming towards us.

Except when we stood watch, we wore shorts and a pair of heavy wooden soled sandals. The sandals had to be thick soled because of the hot metal deck. In the afternoon the deck was so hot you could almost fry an egg on it.

March 22, 1945

We varied our course eleven times finally beaching at Ormoc, Leyte, the other side of island from Tacloban. We had 250 men aboard from Company M and HO (a code name for a general we had on board) 40th Division. We had no ground fire.

During this time we had been up and down the coast of Luzon Subie Bay, Lingayen Gulf and Clark Field. I enjoyed talking with the fighter pilots at Clark Field. In their minds they were the best and they proved it over and over again. In my opinion, if it hadn't been for the Kamikaze planes the war would have been over by this time. If the Kamikazes weren't shot down by ship or airplanes they seldom missed. The longer you saw this suffering and horrible death the more you wondered, will I be next. They were not after a small ship such as an LCI but when they were hit they would take anything in sight.

While in Luzon we had our first liberty. It was the first for me in sixteen months and for the original crew the first in 22 months. Port and starboard each had twelve hours. When starboard failed to show on time, port took off. I was on portside. There wasn't much to see. It was mostly bamboo huts with people sleeping on mats. Jap rice whiskey was available as well as sake, Jap wine. Both were better than the Tumba juice available at Tacloban.

The town we visited was Cavite, just about six miles from Manilla. We could see the lights of Manilla but I don't think anyone went there. It would have been a long walk. People didn't seem that happy to see us in their town. The pictures I have seen on television seem to show the people have not upgraded themselves very much.

There is only one place I would to visit again and that's New Guinea. I would like to see if they upgraded themselves. It is for sure it couldn't be worse.

All these months I had a sub machine gun in the pilot house and on this day I shot 10 rounds at tin cans. What do you know? I missed. I wasn't as good a shot as Clarke.

March 24

We knew something big was coming up and that we were not going to be involved. This was the first island hop since Noemfoor that we hadn't been involved in. We were happy and yet sad. We knew there was more fighting to do before we got to go home.

April 1

The invasion of Okinawa. It almost seemed as we were there, firing at those many Kamikaze planes.

LCI 447 doing its job. Well-trained troops invaded enemy territory ready to give their lives.

*Here I was the first day I landed in New Guinea as a
replacement.*

USS LCI (L) 447
Fleet Post Office
San Francisco, Calif.

2 May 1945

From: Commanding Officer, U.S.S. LCI (L) 447.
To :   COLE, Orest Gilmore, QM 3/c
             Ser. No. 955-27-30, U.S. Naval Reserve.

Subject: Commendation for Services Beyond the Call
             of Duty.

Reference: (a) BuPers manual Article D-8016.

1.   You are commended for significant loyalty and
repeated rendering of service beyond the call of duty while
serving under this command during the period 20 September 1944
to 2 May 1945.

2.   Particular commendation is made of your
helmsmanship during the tropical storm in the Leyte Gulf,
Philippine area, of October 29 - October 30, 1944, during
which period you remained at the helm over long periods
without accepting relief, and handled the wheel in such
a maner and under such adverse conditions of wind and
weather that this command was enabled to bring ship and
personnel through the storm in safety.

3.   In storm and under enemy attack during the
Phillipine Campaign, under unusual conditions of wind and
current, your helmsmanship has been noteworthy. In work
details and in all aspects of ship board life you have
lived up to the highest traditions of the Naval Service.

GOLDSMITH, Jr.

Copy to:
Service Record

*This is the commendation I received for "Services
Beyond the Call of Duty."*

Sometime after April 23 we heard we were going south and we felt sure we would be going to Australia and liberty. We had liberty but it was in New Guinea. We were sent there for new engines for the invasion of Japan.

A Quartermaster stands signal watch on a small ship. When anchored I stood watch four hours and was off eight hours. I upgraded the maps and practiced signal light and semaphore with Roy Vetter. He was better than I of course. His rate was Signalman. Roy could read a light as fast as anyone could send. He just held the light open. By this time I was a Second Class Quartermaster. Mr. Tag couldn't understand why I wasn't studying for First Class. I knew that with a good job with an excellent company and married with two children I wasn't going to make the Navy a career. First Class Quartermaster has to be quite knowledgeable shooting the stars, plotting courses, etc. Mr. Tag wanted everyone to be the best he could be. The training I received from Mr. Tag and Mr. Goldsmith served me well in later life. Both were brave and high on integrity.

June 6

The war in Europe was over. I happened to be on Signal watch when everyone started to put up flags. They read victory. But I didn't think the Japs would surrender this easily. Mr. Tag detached and headed for duty in the U.S. He took uncensored letters with him from all of us.

We continued to drill and play touch football waiting for the new engines.

The battle was still raging on Okinawa in early June. We heard on June 19, 1945 that Japs were surrendering by the hundreds and dying by the thousands. Rumor had it they had flown 1900 suicide missions, many more than we had seen in the Phillipines.

August 6

We heard a powerful new type bomb had been dropped by a B29.

August 15

I was on signal watch when again the victory flags were run up. I tell you the LCI 447 was not the last ship in the harbor to run up the victory flag. We had a half month's beer ration aboard and didn't wait for it to get cold. We drank it warm.

I had my points in and being married with children and a job to go to I was, I think, the first one transferred to the island for transportation home. We were there for a week waiting for transportation. It seemed like years.

I remember that trip home very clearly. Steak, yes steak, no mutton, was available three times a day if we liked. I had my fill as did everyone. We shot crap and played cards. Once I had a little over $1,800, a lot of money in those days. After a while another man and I had all the money. Like a fool, I played him head to head; he got hot and broke me. I switched dice several times and stopped his roll, but he just kept rolling sevens and elevens and then his points. I lost all my money.

To take advantage of the currents we went north where the weather was cold and I, as well as many other men, got terrible colds. Where was PHM 1/C Tucker then?

We were very, very happy when we went under the Golden Gate Bridge. Cheers went up. We went through Treasure Island and then on to Chicago by train. Herman Eckrich was on the same train and when he saw me he came over and said he hoped I would return to work for them adding, ''We need young men like you.'' In those days company officials rode trains not company-owned planes as they do now.

At the Chicago train station I purchased a clown doll for each of my daughters. I'm quite sure one still has her doll. My wife and girls were at the train station. We walked home to where we lived on East Wayne Street. My daughters were both very young when I left, and they did not recognize me. That was the only sad part of my return.

These are true stories taken from ship's log of the invasions of Noemfoor and the Phillipines. Take it from me, war is hell and the next one will put this one to shame.

Some of my readers might wonder why I mention the Skipper S.W. Goldsmith Jr. and LT. JGH Tatgenhorst so often. It's because I worked with them closely under all adverse conditions. At the helm I took direct orders from the Skipper. As for Mr. Tag, he knew how to guide a raw recruit plus I could see him on deck as he lowered the ramp on the invasions and knew by the way he handled himself he was a brave man. I am sure many of the other officers and men were just as good at their jobs.

I did not know that Lt. Schlosser was one of the owners of Schlossers Ice Cream Companies, the largest ice cream company in that day. He was as common as an old shoe.

George Covington was the best poker player on board. When we needed a loan we went to George. We called him Mr. Solid Citizen; he was black.

CHAPTER 7

I started back to work immediately with Eckrich. Since we still had little to sell, they put me on as a relief salesman. This was a break for me. I was able to see how each man approached selling. Joe Eckrich, the youngest son, was no longer a driver salesman. He was now an officer. When I was working nights I had loaded Joe Eckrich's sales truck. Joe Helmkamp was still General Sales Manager. John Norton was the district manager.

Meat was still scarce so we just divided it among all customers. I recall one company that did business the easy way. They sold as much as the customer wanted and then went home. When meat was plentiful they were out of business in a short time. I was the first to be furloughed so I was the last to be put back on my route.

We were still working five and a half days and there were still no locks on the truck doors. We serviced some customers twice a day. A & P was the only supermarket in Fort Wayne. Kroger and Rogers were neighborhood stores. There was no packaged merchandise, everything was bulk. Every Wednesday A & P would take a truck load for the weekend.

One Saturday morning a storm came up suddenly and quickly developed into a downpour. The underpasses were flooded in minutes. I drove into one of them but couldn't see because the glass was steamed up. About midway through I stalled. Due to my lack of experience I didn't try to use the battery to get me through.

A group of youngsters were having a ball in the water. I gave the largest one fifty cents to carry me out on his shoulders to the elevated sidewalk. Even though I expected to be fired, no one said a word. They scrapped the meat I had in the truck. Then they put a new engine in the truck as the cinders had plugged it. Also the inside of the truck had to be thoroughly cleaned and varnished. Eckrich stood head and shoulders above any other food company in cleanliness.

Shortly after this happened Harold (Hack) Mosel purchased a truck-stop just outside LaGrange, a town he serviced on his Tuesday run. Hack had taught me on my present route and told John Norton, the District Manager, that I would do a good job on this route so John gave me the job. This route was made up of two areas. I went to Garrett, Avilla and Kendalville on Monday, Wednesday and Thursday, an 80-mile round trip. On Tuesday and Friday I drove 210 miles to Wolcottville, LaGrange, Middleburg, Topeka, Ligionier and a number of other small towns.

May I tell you how business was operated in those days, and how people treated a salesperson. We didn't do much business in Garrett until Nate Haffel gave me a break and started to advertise. What a grand old man he was.

Jim Koon was the Northern Indiana Democratic Chairman and an important man in Indiana politics. He treated me like a member of his family, red meat, steaks, and so forth were still scarce, but Jim made sure I had plenty of steaks. My wife prepared me a steak for me every night. After mutton in the Navy, this was a real treat.

My first stop in Kendallville wasn't open when I went by, so rather than have me backtrack, the store owner gave me a key. He signed a blank check to Eckrich and I filled in the amount and left him his bill. If we could just go back to those days of trust. I took my own order in all except one store in Kendalville. Eckrich had over 95% of all lunch meat business in town.

After a few months on the LaGrange run I started to service a bakery with a number of bread routes called huckster routes. These drivers wanted to leave around 6:00 am and since LaGrange was 60 miles north of Fort Wayne, two days a week I had to leave the plant at 4:30 am. These bakery routes sold a few other staple goods. They were good customers. I would run all day on this route. I was in terrific shape.

In those days there was no packaged merchandise. You went into the store, took the order, went out to the truck, got the merchandise, went back into the store, weighed, billed and collected for the merchandise. I was selling about 20,000 pounds a week. There were no shopping carts. You carried the merchandise in a wire basket. The Topeka, Middleburg, LaGrange, and Ligoniere areas were mostly populated by Amish people. They were very conservative, but liked good food and Eckrich had the best.

Meat markets like John Mischler's purchased ring bologna by the bushel basket. John would leave one to twelve baskets on the back step. I would sell him ten to thirty large bolognas, five to twenty-five six-pound boxes of franks, one or two honey loaves and one or two pickle loaves.

The teaching of my Mother and Aunt Ann served me well in this job. I respected my customers and serviced them to the best of my ability. They trusted me and treated my family well. Some would visit us on Sunday. We were able to buy a new home in a good neighborhood. We even replaced our old Chevy which we had purchased from a junk yard years before for $25.00. Our daughters were going to school in Fort Wayne. By this time we also had two sons.

The company was growing and expanding. In those days it seems management selected management personnel by choosing the top salesperson. For about three years I never finished below third place, tonnage-wise. I was in first place most of the time. When the company decided to open a new district in Brazil, I was offered the job of District Manager even though I was not the smartest or most qualified man. I bid my customers good-bye and broke in my replacement. Then the Korean War broke out and the company didn't know if there was going to be another meat shortage so I was put back on the old route. The company was non-union at this time and employees did not want to join so the union shut off our fresh meat supply and forced us to join. The company was one of the largest users of fresh picnics in the world. Pork makes the best lunchmeat and picnics the most flavorful. This cut is not popular in the home because of the fat and gristle. The company boned the picnics in four parts taking out the fat and gristle.

The Company decided to open the Brazil district the day after Labor Day, 1951. Our youngest daughter said, "Dad, I won't move unless we move to the country and you buy me a horse." Since I was born on a farm I thought this was a good idea. Of course, our horses were mules on the farm. We couldn't find a suitable home near Brazil, so we moved to a very old home in Stanton. What a let down for my family.

John Norton, my old boss, and I went to Brazil and hired two salesmen. The comptroller hired what we called a chief clerk. She was to check invoices for errors, file, etc. Working the long hours I had worked I had never seen the office girls in Fort Wayne unless they came in on a Saturday. In fact I knew little about running an office.

Our oldest daughter stayed with her grandparents the summer of 1951 knowing she would not get to see them very often after the move. Her first week in school she became ill. The doctor said polio and they kept her a week at Brazil's hospital. My wife stayed with her days, I stayed nights. I would leave the hospital at 5 AM, shower, shave and be back at the district at 6 AM. Each day I would ride with the salesman driving the farthest before his first stop. I slept until the first stop. I never missed visiting the store with the salesman and would sleep after the last stop until we got to the plant. I doubt if anyone knew Jo had polio that week. I didn't think people would want to be exposed to someone who had been exposed to polio. We then took her to Riley Hospital in Indianapolis. The chief doctor said "Take her home, she is a hopeless cripple." We were not satisfied with this. In my travels I got to talk to lots of different people around the area and someone told me about a retired osteoplastic surgeon in Champaign, IL. At the time there were only two in the state of Illinois. We took Jo to this doctor and she accepted the challenge.

So we started taking Jo to her twice a week. I went with my wife and Jo every Saturday. This doctor believed all the muscles were controlled by nerves in the back of the head. One of Joe's legs was completely paralyzed and it was cold as ice. We must have visited the doctor twice a week for a year before Jo felt any warmth or feeling in her leg. At first, she felt the warmth for just a few seconds, then it lasted minutes, then hours, then days. Then for weeks her leg stayed warm. We called this beating the odds. Jo improved after this, day by day.

There were 35 homeowned stores in Terre Haute all related. When these people learned Eckrich was a respectable company with a good product and only one price list they accepted us. Terre Haute was our largest town. The area had one major chain—Kroger. I had never called on a chain buyer before but I knew we had to get this chain if we were to succeed in this area. I was nervous. Here I was, someone a school teacher at Harmor School in Fort Wayne, IN had once called a "southern Indiana washout," calling on a person with huge responsibilities. For a chain buyer to take on a product that was new to the area takes nerve because it could cost him his career.

Before trying to sell them I found out about their likes and dislikes and their needs. I didn't know about features, benefits, trial closes, closes, etc. then. Years later I knew I had done this my entire career without knowing it.

Kroger had moved a grocery merchandiser into Terre Haute about the time Eckrich opened the Brazil branch. His name was Gail Blakeley. We met and became friends. We corresponded after we both left the area until he passed on about 30 years later. What a terrific man Gail was.

Kroger, was creating supermarkets out of Mom and Pop stores. I was able to sell Buck Mills, the Kroger merchandiser, on Eckrich merchandise and helped them open stores. I did whatever Buck or Gail wanted me to do such as set meat cases, wash cases, weigh ground beef etc. The stores were open 9 to 9 then. We were there at 7:00 AM to set up the meat department and would stay until 11:00 PM. On Saturday evening from about midnight until 7:00 AM Sunday we played poker at someone's house. After Kroger opened all the supermarkets they had planned for the area Buck and Gail were transferred to Indianapolis.

Gail and Buck were very good friends. They called me John as they didn't like my first name, Orest.

Busy as I was opening new routes and working with Kroger on openings, the only time I was in the office was Saturday morning. We had no relief salesmen at that time. When a salesman was absent the District Manager ran his route. If the night loader was absent, I loaded the trucks.

The only time I ever saw the Chief Clerk was if she came to the office on Saturday morning. One day she came in and said, "would you hire my boyfriend?" I agreed to talk to him. He came in. He was 42. I let him down as easy as possible but I didn't hire him. I was looking for big young men in their early twenties. If I made a good choice I knew they would be good employees for years. They had to be tall men so they could reach the top shelf without stepping on the truck steps. And they had to be young. At 42 I knew her boyfriend could not stand working 12 to 14 hours at low pay. In established areas the pay was much better than the average job but in new areas our salesmen did not make good money. After he left she came in. To this day I can still see her. I bet she jumped a foot off the floor with fire in her eyes. She would hardly speak to me after that when I called the office.

One day the General Sales Manager asked me to stay at the district office the next day. My boss, Joe Helmkamp, a religious, honest man, arrived and the Comptroller was with him. They questioned me at length on my office duties. When they left we had no Chief Clerk. She was terminated. She had told the comptroller I was never at the office and I wasn't working. She was trying to get me fired. When I heard these things my Irish temper let the comptroller have it. Later my boss said he appreciated the way I stood up to the comptroller. He then said, "No one is going to fire my people unless I am present."

Like anything, if you are exposed often enough to any danger you will have some close calls or see some accidents, especially in a truck. I liked to ride with a salesman two or three times on the same route to show him some sales pointers. I was riding with Ken Hood on his Friday route and the first stop was Clinton, IN. Just off Highway 41. Highway 41 was a two-lane highway from Chicago to Florida and was very busy in those days. The driver of the car in front of us couldn't make up his mind where to go and Ken bumped him in the rear ever so slightly. We exchanged the names of our insurance companies and the people in the other car said there were no injuries. I insisted they go to the hospital in Clinton for a checkup and the checkups were negative. The next week they sued the Company for $10,000. This was well before the days of the million dollar lawsuits.

The following Friday I rode with Ken again. We turned off 41 going to Covington and stopped to service a store about two blocks off 41 when a firetruck went by at full speed with firemen standing on the sides. One of us said that if they didn't slow down, there would be an accident. They didn't and there was an accident—a bad one. Several firemen were seriously injured. The firetruck had run the stop sign and gone under a cattle truck going north on highway 41.

The next Friday, I rode with Ken again on the same route. Just before we came to Fowler, there is, or should I say was at the time, a two lane bridge. A large stone truck going south and small gravel truck going north collided. We were two vehicles back. It was a close call. When they pulled the man from the small gravel truck the gravel had shifted onto the cab. There wasn't any blood but his body was like a bowl of jelly. It looked as if every bone in his body had been crushed and, of course, he was dead. Next Friday, I said to Ken, ''No way am I riding with you.'' His comment, ''I knew you weren't. If you were I was taking the day off.''

CHAPTER 8

We moved into a remodeled home outside Brazil and Judy got her horse, a pinto mare. I liked horses but had never been around one as we had mules on the farm. The place where we purchased the mare had a bay quarter horse stud. I told the owner I would buy the mare if he would breed her.

When I made the purchase I took along my neighbor, Mr. Martin. He was approaching 65 and had no Social Security, so for two years he rode one of his horses three miles each way to work to qualify for Social Security. Mr. Martin was the best horseman I every knew. He knew Appy, the nickname for Appaloosa, was going to be a popular color and he bred for one. Judy's mare, Lady, had a foal and Judy named the filly Friskey. She was palamino in color.

Mr. Martin made a real pet out of his Appy filly. It would give you a kiss, shake hands and tell you how old it was by stomping a foot. When it was time to break Friskey, I tied two sacks of grain across the saddle, one on each side. These sacks when full bumped against her legs. At day's end she would no longer be scared. I also neck reined her at the same time. After a couple of days I got on her back and she did not buck once.

One day Mr. Martin told me he was going to break the filly. Since he was over 65, I told him I was no horseman but to let me break her. I got in the saddle but the filly didn't move. She just stood there stiff-legged, glassy eyes rolling. For some reason Mr. Martin cracked her across the rump with a leather strap and she took off like a shot. The fence was only about 25 yards away and I had to pull her up. When I did that she went over backwards with me. If a horse has never gone over backwards with you, take it from me it's a long way to the ground. I rolled away from the saddlehorn, and I said "This is enough for me today."

The next day was Sunday and I asked Mr. Martin to let me have the filly so that I could break her like I did Friskey. He agreed. I took her and threw the two empty sacks over the saddle. They were slapping against her legs when being filled and she was doing fine. I had relaxed as she seemed okay. Then suddenly she reared up on her hind legs and came after me striking at me with her front legs and snapping at me with her teeth. I fell down stumbling on the corn stalks. I kept rolling around out of her way until she settled down. I took her home, and told Mr. Martin that she was dangerous. He sold her and the buyer came after her in a new pickup truck. She went up over the cab and down over the hood. They had to walk her to their place. The last I heard she was going blind from people beating her over the head trying to break her from going over backwards.

I had Friskey bred to a good American Saddlebred Palomino stallion. Friskey was a two-year-old at the time.

The next spring Friskey had her foal, a pale cream palomino. Judy named her Beauty. There was one big problem. It seems I had Friskey bred too young and she would not claim the foal or let it nurse. I guess this is very rare, about one in a million. Friskey hated the foal and would have killed it. The foal seldom lives when this happens because although a foal takes little milk at time, it nurses very often. The vet made up a special formula for Judy to feed the filly. Judy fed this little thing every half hour for three weeks. It not only survived but grew quite quickly. It was a people's animal and Friskey still hated it. Beauty would have gladly come into the house with us if we had let her.

The boys, Mike and Brent, were not fond of horses and wanted other pets. We got them two small chickens which turned out to be two roosters. They were both mean as dirt as the boys had teased them while they were growing up. We named them Pete and Repete. Our neighbors, the Sterleys, had a cat who had kittens and then was killed shortly after. I found the nest in their barn and one kitten was still alive. I took it home. The kids fed it first with an eye dropper and then with a bottle and nipple as it grew. About the same time, a salesman, Ken Hood, ran over a mother coon that had babies. One survived. I took it home and the kids named it Cooney. Cooney and Kit Cat both had bottles and were fed at the same time. We also had a Cocker Spaniel named Buttons. They were all friends. The coon and kitten played like two kittens. All were housebroken. Cooney was an excellent pet. Cooney would play with the kids by the hours.

Our driver salesmen were still not making big money as it takes time to build a brand name even with the best product. My old boss John Norton said, "Opening new territory is like having cancer, it just keeps gnawing away at you." I asked the salesmen to work long hours and at low pay so naturally we had quite a turnover. One man had been seeing me each week for months for a job. Even though I knew little about hiring, my gut feeling told me he would not work out. He was over thirty, a success in his field and well known in the area. One day I needed a man and had no good prospects to hire. I hired this man. I worked with him two weeks and the third week he started alone. At noon he called the district saying, "Will you come and finish the route? This job is not what I thought it would be." My instinct was correct. Back in those days I believed if someone was going to be a success he would be on his way at 30.

I looked for big men who had played sports in high school. I thought if they had played sports they were coachable. I wasn't interested in anyone who had been in sales. I was interested in teaching them my way. I believe it is hard to teach an old dog new tricks, plus if someone had been successful why would he be interested in this job.

When I was young it seemed a salesperson had to be a good story teller and know many jokes. This was not what I was looking for in a salesmen. I was interested in hiring an honest young man with goals. To this day I can't tell or remember a joke.

Jo was now a senior at Brazil High and Judy was a sophomore. Jo was chosen homecoming queen and Judy was the princess. We were proud parents. The average person couldn't tell

Jo had had polio. But one of her legs was not quite as large around as the other and she had what is called a drop foot. All this time Eckrich was only state inspected, since they only sold in Indiana and Michigan where they had plants. Now they were making plans to go for federal inspection. They selected Ohio as the first state to open with Findlay, Ohio, as the first district. Since this city was close to my hometown of Antwerp, Ohio, I asked for the position. They thought I was nuts for going through all that hard work again but Joe Helmkamp thought I deserved the opportunity.

My replacement in Brazil was Joe Quinlan, a man much more intelligent than I. After several years he became president and then chairman of the company. Years later, Joe told me one of the men said when he first arrived, "If you are going to be like that other fellow, tell me now so I can quit."

I don't think I did a good job in Brazil. I didn't know how to manage people. I worked like hell and don't think I ever asked anyone to do anything I wouldn't do myself. We had good people and a good product, so the company grew. Years later one of the men who I as sure didn't like me said, "You were one of two of the best bosses I ever had," adding. "You never lied to me." A wealthy supermarket owner told me the same thing. I'm quite sure all the men who stayed with the company prospered and became solid citizens of Brazil. Two of them, Larry Parr and Ken Ramey, joined the Eckrich management team.

Prior to opening the Findlay district I helped train Fort Wayne personnel who would be selling our product in Ohio. One of them was a young man by the name of Ursell Cox. He was just a youngster when I serviced his family's store in Kendallville, IN. When I introduced ourselves in stores most people blinked, adding, "Where did your company find people with such odd names?"

Our daughter Jo was now attending Indiana University when she was doing well. Judy was elected queen at Brazil High School as a Junior. At the time we were the only parents to have two daughters elected queen. If I may say so, we were quite proud and naturally thought they were pretty.

When school was out I moved the family to Findlay including horses, dog and cat. Cooney had stayed with us until full grown and then I assume he joined other coons. Judy pastured her horses at the Spitler's.

Judy's filly had never been stabled. When winter came it gets very cold in Findlay so she put lots of bedding in her stall. The filly was nervous and pawed the bedding away from the corner of the stall. She lay in this corner and threw her neck out. We couldn't get her to stand up. We lifted her by pulleys and she would fall back down. Finally I found a vet who suggested I talk her up. I got down by her and started talking to her in a gentle voice and in about a minute she got up on her own and was not frightened. But her neck was bent in almost a ''u'' shape. She looked terrible but did not seem to be in any pain.

I contacted vets all over northern Ohio including Ohio State University. No one knew what to do. Finally I located a vet in Decatur Indiana who took her, but when he put the neck back into place it killed her because her neck had fused. I tell you this was a sad day in the Cole family. She was a terrific pet and a beautiful horse.

We returned to Brazil the next summer so the kids could see their friends. When we visited the Martins Mr. Martin told Judy all you had to do was throw the filly down, throw a rope around its neck and pull the neck back in place. He knew more than the vets knew in Northern Ohio plus those at Ohio State University.

I am sure leaving Brazil when she was a senior was very hard for Judy. The boys adjusted very well and they had friends the next day.

CHAPTER 9

We opened the district in May. I did the hiring and Eugene (Bud) Eckrich came down from Michigan to help me open it. Our schedule was breakfast at 6 AM and dinner at 10PM. Bud was terrific and asked for no quarter. He carried his share of the work. Even though we worked for the same company and followed the same operating directions no two people sell alike. We didn't want to confuse the young salesmen so each one of us stayed with the same salesman while training him. Bud helped me on, and off, for about six months.

The Findlay district grew rapidly for three reasons: excellent merchandise, terrific young salesmen and outstanding office personnel. Rumor was that Ruth Sharp, Chief Clerk, Helen Sands and Shirley Spaeth were the best district office personnel in the company. Probably the most important factor in our growth was the merchants in northwestern Ohio. These merchants knew good merchandise and enjoyed offering it to their customers. Normally a larger city such as Toledo is harder to develop than a small town. This was not so in Toledo's case.

I had less turnover in salesmen because I was smarter about hiring. Most stayed with the company in Findlay until they were promoted or found better positions. I gave each a nickname and listed below are a few. Gene Cramer (Jumbo) big tummy then, not now, (2) Gene Lauber (Lube), (3), Bob Cole, no relation (Big Time). He came to work the first day in a big old Caddy. It looked to me like it was a block long. I named him Big Time after the big car, (4 Jerry Bach (Mias), (5) Don Crawford (Bigem), I weighed 175 and he weighed exactly 100 pounds more, (6) Bob

Huffman (Huff), (7) Duane Heck (Heckle Jeckle & Hide). He always tried to hide when I was looking for him, (8) Kent Props (Propsey), (9) Wayne Sheets (Paper), he was paper thin when he started, (10) Gary Spaeth (Speedy), (11) Wes Crabiel (Westy), (12) Don Kemmerly (Don A. Hue), (13) Robert McLain (Mac A Doodle Dandy), (14) Baxter Boyle (Bax), (15) Bill Hemmer (Billy the Kid), (16) Ron Rahe (Roxey) solid as a rock, (17), Joe Brodey (Brodie). I had to be a little nuts to give people names like this. They were a hard working, fun loving bunch. They worked together and played together. When I hired Bob Cole, I got a telephone call from my boss, John Norton. His first word was, "Orest." I immediately knew I was in trouble as no one called me Orest and John always called me "Coley." "Orest," he said, "What the hell are you breaking company policy for. You know you can't hire your relatives." I told him Bob was no relative—just another English American.

I had another unusual experience about this time. I got a phone call from Dave Reel, one of the salesmen, who was on vacation. Dave said, "I am going to play golf at McComb, please join me." I told him I had too much work to do. I thought many times I might have saved Dave's life if I had joined him as no doubt his schedule would have been different. Dave was hit broadside in his car on his way home.

Summer was golf and fishing, fall and winter it was football at Findlay College. The wives suffered I am sure, I know mine did. Their satisfaction was that their husbands made well above average incomes. Ron Rahe, Joe Brodie, Bill Hemmer and I played golf every Saturday for I am sure over five years. We played from 18 to 36 holes. My partner was the best and I was the worst. We played $5.00 a nine, but at the end of the year we lost no more than $100.00.

One day at McComb we were two strokes behind for the 18. They were all on the green and I needed an eagle to tie. I was about thirty yards to the left of the green and about five yards above. The green was on a steep hill. It's for sure they would need two putts to get down in the cup. I chipped and the ball went into the cup. It was the first and only eagle I ever made. We played 27 holes for the tie off. They beat us badly thanks to me. I couldn't do anything right the next nine. Roxey had been a little all American football player at Findlay College. He was big and strong. Brodie had been an outstanding defensive back. One of the ways we beat these guys is I would say, "Now we will watch Rox hit the ball 300 yards." After this Rox would wind up and hit the ball 300 plus yards and usually out of bounds.

About this time, Joe Helmkamp retired. What a terrific man he was and how nice he was to work for. John Norton was made General Sales Manager. John was the best pure salesman I ever saw. I will mention him again later.

The chain merchandisers and buyers were good to us in Toledo as were the supermarket owners, news media, newspapers, radio and television. I remember my first time on television. The company introduced a processed beef loaf very similar to dried beef. I introduced it on Toledo television for the area. I was almost as scared then as I was under battle conditions in the South Pacific. An elderly gent with the Toledo grocery association ran a feature for us about every week. He was a great help.

The salesmen belonged to the Teamsters Union and a fellow by the name of Frank ran the Toledo Union. He sat in on some of our meetings. He said the salesmen curse you but in the same breath say no one else had better. When I left the area, Frank wrote me a nice letter.

I remember the chain buyers in the Terre Haute and Toledo area because I knew if Eckrich was to be a success we had to sell these accounts. I spent more time with them and got to know them better than some of the other customers I called on in later years.

I'm quite sure many people believe that people in high positions demanded gifts, money or favors of some sort for authorization of store position, ads, etc. I can say, in all my years, no one asked for any gift or ever expected any from me. They wanted something that would sell and satisfy their customers.

My only hope is that our government officials have the same high standards as these people. If they do, our country is in good shape.

I'd like to acknowledge some of the Toledo, Columbus and Pittsburgh people who helped me a great deal and who played a big part in my life, beside my wife, my Mother and my Aunt: Larry Askrin, Dial Baher, Wayne Christerson, Walter Churchill, Sr., Joel Greenhisen, Bill Johnstone, Mac McCarthy, Joe Slagle, Frank Ulrich, Don Spalding, Cliff Smith and Tommy Vaughn. All these were very important people in their field.

Joel Greenhisen just graduated from Ohio State and started to work as a meat buyer in Columbus Ohio for Kroger and I was the first salesperson to call on him. Joel was V.P. of Kroger in Louisville, KY, the last I heard of him. Some twenty years latter I was in the Atlanta airport and I heard someone say, "Orest, (no one calls me Orest) if you have a minute, I would like you to meet my family." Joel and his family were returning from a Florida vacation. I thought it was terrific that after all these years Joel wanted me to meet his family.

Cliff Smith advanced from store employee to VP. at A&P, Pittsburgh. Cliff had the vision to know Eckrich would do well in Pittsburgh. With Wes Crabiel's hard work along with Cliff's support we grew. The company now has a district in Pittsburgh and the last I heard it is one of Eckrich's best districts.

What a man Walter Churchill, Sr. is. We had an Operation Direction which says we hire no employees from other stores unless we get permission from the owner or chain. Dick Abbott who worked for Churchill's applied for a sales position. I paid Walter Sr. a visit to get his permission. Walter Sr. is the only man in the Marines who went from a private to General in World War II. Here I was, a Quartermaster Second, talking to a General who owned supermarkets in the Toledo area. He in no uncertain terms, told me not to hire Dick Abbott. His wife overheard. He was a large well muscled man and his wife was small but firey. She joined us and her first words were, "Sr., you are talking against everything you believe in. What are you going to do for

Dick Abbott? All you can do is make him a meat manager!''
Churchill Sr. said, ''You are right,'' and gave me permission to
hire Dick.

I named Dick (Dickie DO) and he went on to a management
position with Eckrich and then General Sales Manager with the
Owens Sausage Co. in Texas.

I had a horrible time selling Oscar Joseph, Jr. I'm quite sure
I called on him for more than a year before selling him one
pound. When I finally got his confidence I got a customer and a
friend. The company grew rapidly with them. The Joseph family
was in all kinds of businesses in Toledo—you name it and they
were in it. I had lunch with Jr. at 1 PM each Tuesday. If I took
another customer to lunch I had two lunches that day. One day
Jr. said, ''Cole, my brother Georgia isn't selling many hot dogs
at his K.F.C. stores. Would you object if I asked him to join us
for lunch?''

Well, all through lunch George kept saying our prices were
too high, and I kept saying we had the best so we were higher.
Pretty soon Jr. said, ''Georgie, buy those hot dogs or shut up.
You're talking to Cole and he is giving you his best price.'' I
can't say how proud I was when I heard this.

After Findlay I was promoted to Regional Manager. We
opened Cleveland, Columbus and Cincinnati. The company was
not ready to open Pennsylvania at this time. It takes time and
money to open new territories. We then opened Akron; Acme
was the major chain in the area. Pete Kessler was the merchandiser. Mr. Kessler gave us the opportunity to service their stores
through their warehouse.

When we were ready to sell to the chains in Columbus other
than Kroger (we were already in Kroger) we planned a all-day
meeting for each chain. The first day we were getting no place
with the chain we were trying to sell. In fact the merchandiser
we had to sell shook us up around 11 AM when he started to
snore. At lunch John Norton advised all Eckrich personnel that
he was scrapping our entire program. During the lunch hour John
organized a completely new program that turned out to be a

complete success. In his day, John had to be the best pure sales-person with the best vision of a customer's needs in the country.

On Friday, July 26, 1959, I was returning from Bellefoun-taine, Ohio, after seeing Bill Johnstone, with Super Foods, IGA. On the trip home I had a terrible accident. I was within a mile of the city limits when two cars going south collided. One piled into the car ahead of it and then bounced over into my lane hitting me head-on. The fellow who hit me had a big Caddy. I was driving an Oldsmobile.

I remember trying to get up right after the accident but then I fainted. I was not expected to live and they did not set any bones for a week. I was unconscious for six days except for brief periods. When I did regain consciousness I thought I was dying. Why? Where I was raised people died at home and I had heard what they call the death rattle. When I was conscious briefly I heard what I thought was a death rattle. I was scared. Believe me this was a chilling thought. I then relaxed thinking that if I am going to be taken by God there is nothing I can do, but if I do have a chance I must relax and fight. Thought about my four youngsters that I was responsible for. I found out later the gear shift had gone through my neck and punctured my windpipe. I was breathing through this hole. I was told that is the only way I had survived as my throat had swollen shut. Doctors told me it was pure luck that my windpipe was punctured.

I had lots of company at the hospital. The salesmen smug-gled in beer every evening. But I did have one bad experience. I was barely conscious when an insurance salesman came into my room and tried to get me to sign off. Even then there were some crooks. I wasn't conscious enough to know who he repre-sented. My face was completely smashed in and my family did not recognize me when they came into my hospital room. I under-stand another 1/32 of an inch and my skull would have damaged my brain. I had a fractured skull along with broken ribs.

It wasn't until months later that I had plastic surgery. There were no plastic surgeons in Findlay and I had to go to Columbus.

The surgeon was very popular and I heard he averaged four operations a day. He took bone from my hip, ground it, split my gums around the teeth I had left and put it up between my teeth and cheekbone to build up the face. My nose was flat against my face and he took a crowbar (yes a crowbar) and pried my nose away from my skull. I couldn't believe what I saw the next day in the mirror. My head looked like a bowling ball. For eyes there were two slits, for the nose two slits to breath through, and the mouth was a thin line. They fed me through tubes. My face was completely black and blue when the bandages were removed. The doctors did a fine job; however I preferred the way I looked before the accident. I don't care for the pug nose I now have. One is never the same after a severe accident and I will have aches and pains for the rest of my life.

Dr. Tille rebuilt my right elbow and knee. I have a Tille-made knee and elbow and he was proud of the job he had done.

The fellow who hit me was wealthy and hired the best attorneys in the area. The fellow he ran into had $10,000 insurance, nothing else. We split the $10,000—$5,000 each, my attorney's fees took most of the $5,000.

Later in life I had many safety meetings for my salespeople. A number of times the State Police attended. Without mentioning any names I would describe my accident. To the men they would say that the second driver was traveling too close. The important thing to me was that I lived and was able to support and raise my family. Eckrich paid me a full salary while I was off which was nice of them.

Watching safety films I have learned that two cars coming together at 50 miles per hour is the same as falling off a ten story building in a car. The police estimated we each were doing 50 miles at the time of impact. We were both in heavy cars and lived.

The company prospered under Federal inspection. They transferred Bud Lill (I called him Bear) from Shipping Superintendant in Fort Wayne, to Kalamazoo to be Superintendent of all shipping. I had skinned hot dogs alongside Bud in the late 30's. We used strong rubber bands to secure the lids on the frankfurt box when it was full and weighed. I had flipped a few rubber bands at Bud in those days. Our foreman Petie Glenn, a small, easy going boss, usually pretended not to see us having a little horse play. Those bands did sting however. The Bear did me many favors. Others in shipping did not seem to understand my problems in the new areas. Bud said, "You sell it and we will make it."

After Akron I went to Youngstown Ohio, where we serviced Loblaw's chain. From there, to Buffalo, then Syracuse, New York, servicing A&P and Loblaw out of their warehouses. We started to hire women as field merchandisers. We had Bernice in Buffalo and Mary in Syracuse. They were demonstrating a variety of products on Friday and Saturday in stores when I observed them. I liked what I saw and hired them. They didn't know the meat business but they knew they were selling something better than they had ever sold before. What loyal employees they were.

The Company went public in 1962 or 1963. I borrowed money and purchased stock. I knew the Company was going to grow at a more rapid pace. I paid this debt off and borrowed more to purchase more stock. The Company was growing so fast they ran out of funds and Eckrich sold to Beatrice Foods. Soon after the sale both Richard and Donald Eckrich joined the Beatrice management team as officers. Joe Quinlan was made company president.

Don Menze opened the company military operations along with a sales district in Washington, D.C. He had done a nice job and was made a Regional Manager.

Bernice and Mary were doing a good job in Buffalo and Syracuse. I have to say I felt they were doing better than a man would have done. These women did not get discouraged. If you think selling an unknown product in a new area isn't hard, try it sometime. You make the sale, go back the next trip a week or so later and find a half pound package has sold. The meat manager is really unhappy. What do you do now? This isn't a football game and you can't punt nor can you run and hide. You smile and convince him to let you put up some point of purchase material, cut up some samples and sample it out to sell the product. Day after day, hour after hour, they did this sort of thing. Most meat salesmen would have become discouraged, not these women.

There were some fun times. I played a round of golf with a chain buyer in Buffalo, a beautiful course. I saw deer on the course. Another time I spent a day with a merchandiser in Syracuse and we had dinner. He said, "It's early, let's go to a show." This man was single and religious with a fine background. I was shocked when I found the show was a high-class strip joint. I was shocked again when the girls came over to our table and called this man by name. He said he visited the place frequently and called them artists. I don't think he paid any attention to their bodies, but you can bet I did. Another time a merchandiser with one of the chains insisted I stay the weekend for a seafood party. If you have never spent any time at a New England seafood bash please do so. This merchandiser had just authorized our line in his chain and he wanted me to present the line to other management people. Authorizing a new unknown line of product into a chain is a big decision for a merchandiser to make. Its a great opportunity to have a nice display of your product.

The Company decided to open Georgia and start in Atlanta, the hub of the South. I flew down with samples, rented a car and started out, map in hand. Being an ex Quartermaster I used the sun as a guide. Atlanta is an easy town to get around in even for a small town fellow from Antwerp, Ohio. I started making chain contacts—Kroger, A&P, Big Apple, Colonial, and Winn Dixie along with the independent chains who had a warehouse program.

I stayed in a motel and had samples flown in each evening, storing them at a food processor in the city. I cooked sausage each morning with a fry pan in the motel before I started out with the sausage in a thermos jug. This would last until noon and at noon I would eat at a small diner and pay them to cook me more sausage for the afternoon. Why smoked sausage? We had a terrific product. And no smoked sausage was sold in Atlanta.

One evening I came back to the motel dead tired. Without thinking I took a left over piece of sausage and flushed it down the toilet. This caused some excitement as it didn't go down. I changed motels.

I had good success with the chains, and the merchandisers were terrific. They were among the last area merchandisers I got to know real well on a personal basis. As my territory expanded this was the part of the business I missed the most.

Instead of a sales district the company tried something different in Atlanta. We hired foot salesmen who called on the independent stores and we shipped individual store orders to a refrigerated company and they made the delivery. But it didn't work. We decided we knew the driver salesman operation better plus we didn't have the room or equipment to operate in this way.

We opened a sales district in Lithonia, GA. just east of Atlanta. The natives pronounced it Liethnia. Atlanta is in DeCalb County and the natives called it "decab". Lots of southern people had an accent then. Once in a while one would say, "Damn Yankee go home." Now there are few accents and too many Yankees to go home. Atlanta was about one and half million when we opened the district. Ten years later when I left, it was about three million. Bob Williams, Fort Wayne's Special Accounts Supervisor, was made District Manager. We began hiring women field merchandisers on a large scale then. I had to stay for months at the Holiday Inn Airport.

CHAPTER 10

My wife didn't want to live in Atlanta. So we moved just outside the city of Covington and purchased a few acres for the horses. By this time the kids were grown and married. In fact, the youngest was an Eckrich salesman beginning his career. I could get to the airport from Covington faster than if we had lived in northern Atlanta.

John Norton retired as General Sales Manager and Don Menze was now the General Sales Manager, my boss.

I was still living at the Holiday Inn Airport when I got a telephone call from my wife. She said that our son Mike and his wife, Judy, were parents of a baby boy, their second son. She then added he was a Corenlia de lange Child a very rare syndrome. They named him James Arthur. Judy felt this would be an easy name for him to write. Jimmy was born with partial arms and no hands. His inside organs were all reversed. They were advised his intelligence level would not develop beyond the age of one and he was not expected to live beyond the age of five. Today he is twenty-seven and going strong. He is the second person born this way to live this long. In the family it shows what love can do—they love Jimmy and take him everywhere. They call him "Miney Man." He weighs 55 pounds, all chest. The family lives in Largo, Florida, and they are quite athletic. My son Mike and his two other sons referee soccer games on weekends and take Jimmy to all of them. Jimmy is no handicap to the family. He makes them stronger. The kids have many friends who play with and treat Jimmy as an equal. It really is something to see how these young people act around Jimmy when there is no prejudice involved. The athletes who think they are good at sit-ups should see Jimmy do them. He does them as easily as you would raise a hand off the floor.

Jimmy has legs, but no balance and that is the reason he does not stand up. He lies on the floor on his back most of the time. When he wants to go from room to room or anywhere else, he cannot crawl so he rolls.

When John Norton retired, the territories were switched again and I was assigned to Philadelphia and Washington, D.C. I hired Peter Eckrich (fourth generation) who was a route supervisor in the Detroit district to start the Philadelphia area.

I was the only company person Pete saw, so when I was there, Pete and I had breakfast, lunch and dinner together. One day we were at a big hotel downtown. Pete went into the bathroom and didn't return so I ordered for him. The food came and still no Pete so I went to look for him in the restroom. It was a big one. I started walking and yelling, "Pedro!" Where in the heck are you?" I heard no sounds except feet shuffling. I got to the end of the rest room and there was no urinal. All of a sudden I felt about six inches high. I was in the Ladies Restroom. I have never run faster. I got back to the table where Pedro sat eating. I thought he would fall off the chair laughing when I told him my story.

Another time we were on one of Philadelphia's narrow one-way streets. As usual, like all sales people, we were in a hurry. At the end of the block there was a car and a trailer. A man was loading the trailer, and as we approached he started yelling at us to turn around. Pedro kept going. We stopped about 10 yards back. Then Pedro started unwinding out of the car. Let me say right here, Pedro is big. One of his hands is as large as both of mine. This man yelled, "Sorry, I will move." I asked Pedro, "What would you have done if the man hadn't moved"? Without cracking a smile, Pedro said, "We would have had a few fist-cuffs." I had no doubt he would have slugged him. Pete went to college in Philadelphia and he felt right at home there.

Writing about these two incidents brings back some old memories of me getting into trouble. In Brazil, Indiana, Avery Donley and I were playing shuffleboard when a fellow jumped me. I called Avery "Agey." Agey came to the rescue and this fellow and his two pals soon decided they didn't want to have anything to do with the two of us. And one time in Findlay, Bob Huffman and I were sitting in what we called The Tunnel Of Fun, a tavern underground. A man sitting next to me suddenly pulled out a knife and threatened us. I grabbed the knife, which was a cheap one. I broke off the blade and handed the handle back. I said, "If I were you, I would get out of here before I shove this up your—." You should have seen him run.

Another time Bob Cole, no relation, and I were in Fort Wayne. When in Fort Wayne I always visited my Mother. Bob went to Antwerp with me and I dropped him off at my favorite watering hole, The Oasis. When I returned after visiting my Mother, Bob was sitting at the bar. I joined him and we were talking about old times and having a good time. A young man kept butting in on our conversation. He was in his 30's, I was in my 60's. Finally Bob and I moved to a booth to have dinner. But the young man moved over to the booth with us. When I asked him to leave, the man got mad and wanted to fight. I didn't fight for three reasons, (1) I wasn't foolish enough to think I could fight a man half my age, (2) it's for sure I would not embarrass my Mother fighting in my hometown, (3) it was a stacked deck—the brother-in-law of my sister-in-law on my wife's side, owned the tavern. Of course, if I had to fight, Bob probably would have helped me, being big and strong like all the people I hired. I saw him get mad once but instead of slugging the man, he tore a pay telephone off the wall. That took some strength.

We had started out in Washington, D.C. as we had in Atlanta in using foot salesmen to prepared store orders and a refrigerated company to make the deliveries. We had been making the chains in the area for a few years. Ed Hopkins who started as Findlay was a special accounts supervisor. Mike Bilinsky was the District Manager. But the company decided to discontinue this type of operation and put in a sales district with driver salesmen. I took Mike out to dinner my first evening. Mike was young and good looking, a real hell raiser. We were having a few beers and Mike said, "See that pretty girl over there? I am going to take her home." I said to Mike, "She is with another fellow". He said that it didn't matter, he was taking her home. I told him, "If you get into trouble I am not going to help you," He said, "No problem." Mike got up and proceeded to their table. I heard him ask the fellow if the lady was his wife and he was told no. Mike then said, "Your steady girl friend?" "No." Mike said, "Get up, I am taking her home." Darned if the fellow didn't get up and Mike took her home.

We put the district site in Rockville, Maryland in order to service both Washington, D.C. and Baltimore, Maryland with our peddle trucks. Mike supervised both areas; route sales and chain store special account supervisors. This was also the days of the streaker. One of Mike's special account supervisors had an early appointment with a chain merchandiser in Baltimore. Mike stayed in a hotel downtown. The special accounts supervisor stayed with him. Naturally Mike and the supervisor had a couple of drinks. They heard a young lady say, "I am going to streak tonight. I need someone to pick me up in my car in front of the hotel." Do you think Mike would let an opportunity like this slip away? No way. Mike and his friend picked the lady up, people at the hotel got a glimpse of Mike and his friend. As they stepped off the elevators the next morning a couple of fellows yelled, "There are the fellows who picked up the streaker last night." A group gathered around asking questions. This was right up Mike's alley. He was delighted to give them a story.

I helped Mike open Washington and Baltimore as much as I could. I remember how rough Washington D.C. was then, I bet it is terrible now. In those days all the stores were serviced through the alley. Each alley had several toughs meeting us. In new areas we picked up packaged merchandise as it went out of date. These people would beg for merchandise. The product was fine and the vacuum was not broken, it was just out of date so we gave it to them. One day we had no out-of-date merchandise. We told the boys, or men, this and went into the store. When we came out they had ripped off a side door of the truck and taken the entire side of meat products. When the police came, they asked us if we had any names, which we did not. They asked if we had any fingerprints and we told them no. They said, "Nothing we can do," and drove off.

Another time near the Capitol we ran across a new super market having a grand opening which, we had heard, was sponsored by the government. As salespeople we were excited, a new big market just opening. As we pulled into the lot a vehicle pulled up in front of us and stopped. We started to back up to another space but another vehicle pulled in back of us and stopped. We locked the doors and waited. In about a half hour both vehicles pulled away. We did not go into the market.

I had trained or should say helped train a man in Washington, D.C. who seemed like an easy going man. He had a big police dog that he talked about all the time. After awhile he quit the company. A short time later he shot his dog, chased his wife around the neighborhood but couldn't get a good shot at her, so he shot himself.

Ed Hopkins, was seriously injured on a cycle when he ran into a barn while visiting near Findlay. He ran a nail into his skull and they didn't find this out until days later. Although he was partly paralyzed on one side he did a fine job for the company. If fact as of 1994 he hadn't retired. The people at this chain's headquarters thought the world of him.

One day I asked Ed to take some samples to the merchandiser. I said, if he got three new items authorized, the next week we would go to a golf tournament. I went with Ed to see the merchandiser. The merchandiser didn't authorize the items that day but on his next trip he did. So Ed and I went to the golf tournament. It was one of the big ones and we had a ball. I tell his story for one reason—to show that handicapped people can survive and prosper if they put forth the effort. Ed always put forth the effort doing a terrific job and supporting his family.

In new territory you do not make everybody happy all the time. As John Norton used to say, "There are going to be some sheep jump out of the pen." In Baltimore we were servicing a home-owned chain of about eight stores. They were nice stores and we needed them but they dropped our product. I started seeing the merchandiser each week and got to know him quite well. During that time he become ill and went to the hospital for surgery. After surgery I called his wife and when visitors were allowed I visited him but did not try to sell him anything. After he got out he told people at his office, "I couldn't even get sick without this hound running after me." He put us back in his stores.

Bob Williams was making good progress in Georgia. He heard less and less the words "Yankee Go Home." Possibly we should have been more like Ted Turner. Ted Turner claims to be a Southerner and yet if the articles I read are correct, he was born and raised in Cincinnati, Ohio.

When Charles Bayes started out in Findlay, Ohio moved to Georga he didn't know what a horse looked like. Findlay wasn't his hometown and he was young and decided he needed a hobby. He became interested in horses. Gail, his wife, was an avid reader who read every book about horses she could find. Being a hillbilly at the time I hardly knew what a horse gene was but they made a believer out of me about breeding horses. I had sold our horses when we left Findaley and Chuck and Gail convinced us to buy Morgans. In a few short years Chuck and Gail had raised not one but two champion Morgan stallions. They had vets calling them asking what line stallion they should breed their brood mares to.

Judy and her husband came down from New Albany, Indiana on a visit bringing along a Palomino filly. A woman they knew who had just lost her husband and owned the filly and wanted to find a good home for it. The filly's name was Autumn as she was foaled in the autumn and we never changed her name. She was half quarter horse, half American saddle horse breed and she had the gait of the American saddle horse. You get an excellent ride with her. I had purchased a Morgan mare as Chuck and Gail suggested. I did not breed to their stallion as my mare was rather large with big bones. They showed me the stallion I should breed to. He was a fine boned Chestnut with a flax mane and tail. He was beautiful. He was twice a U.S. Champion Morgan. My Morgan mare was coal black and her blood lines dated back to the old U.S. army line. I bred both my mares to this stallion. I bred Autumn to him because I felt since he was a chestnut with a flax mane and tail I was sure to get a golden Palomino. Autumn foaled first and the foal was a roan which we named T.J. after two of our great grandchildren. Her gait was like her dam and she was the prettiest of the four horses. The Morgan was coal black. Her name was Royal Mist but we called her Pepper as she ran all the time. We bred Pepper. She was to foal when my vet was on vacation. He advised me not to worry as he had a vet on standby. I had the feeling Pepper was going to foal one evening so I stayed up. I called the standby vet at 1:00 A.M. You guessed it, he was a no show. I had never seen a mare foal and we were both scared. The foal started to arrive and the horse was scared and got up. I settled her down and she lay down. She had a hard time even thought I was trying to help by pulling on the foal's front legs. It's a wonder any of the three of us survived, but we did. Her name is Misty Nite and we call her Misty.

A couple of years ago, I got a call from Mike Bilinsky. I had called him BoBo Bilinsky and he called me his pen pal as I wrote him many notes. He was laughing as only Mike can laugh. He was thinking about old times and said, I just had to call you and tell you what I did once when I knew you were coming to town. You always said when you came to town, 'Let's visit stores'. I said to myself, I will show him some terrific displays with plenty of point of purchase material. Mike then said, a couple of days later the phone rang and it was the chain supervisor. He was furious and said angrily, "Get over to those stores and take down that Eckrich advertising," adding, "this is not an Eckrich store." In a chain operation we had to get permission from the chain supervisor if we put up point of purchase material. Mike had not asked for permission.

Mike now has the Novus Home Improvement Company in Augusta, Maine. When he called he had 36 employees and was very happy. Mike is one who gets fun out of the life he lives.

The company was still growing but I was spreading myself pretty thin with my supervising. At this time the "Southern Indiana washout" according to the Harmer School teacher in Fort Wayne was having a decent career. But that was about to change for the worse.

A Syracuse grocery chain hired a deli merchandiser from Michigan who was familiar with our product. I had always selected my own people when we started from scratch. This time I did not have this opportunity. The company told me, "You will hire this man." When I hired people I always told them, "I will work as hard for you as I expect you to work for Eckrich. Another thing I always expect is for you to be honest with me." I told him, too. "As we all do, you will make mistakes but if you keep me advised with the truth we will overcome these mistakes." I couldn't give this individual as much help as I would have liked. I watched his orders and they looked good for a new area as they should since we had all the chains' bulk business. I was with this employee and noticed products in the back cooler where the vacuum had blown before it had ever gotten into the deli case. One product has been in their holding cooler so long it was out of date. Bacteria had gotten under the casing causing the vacuum to explode. I knew we were in trouble and went to the chain's warehouse. We had merchandise so far in advance in the warehouse some of the vacuum had blown before it got to the holding cooler at store level. Our employer walked off the job without notice and we lost the account. My hope was the deli merchandiser didn't get in trouble with his employer. It's fore sure the chain, the merchandiser and Eckrich were all big losers.

Anyone who had to travel as much as I did will have a few close calls. One time flying into Buffalo, NY, in the evening, it was snowing and very windy. Just before we got into the terminal, the fellow next to me introduced himself. He said, "I am sure you didn't notice this, but I did as I am a pilot. We came down the runway side ways." He was right. I had not noticed.

The other time was Washington, D.C. on a Friday evening. I was returning home and got to the airport late. As I was boarding I noticed about a half dozen noisy people. You could tell they had been drinking. We started to taxi out but just as we got on the runway there was a very loud bang. The pilot immediately told us not to worry. He said, "Folks, the engine just backfired. We will pull off to the side of the runway and the terminal will have someone pick us up." When returning from a trip I always did one of three things—worked, slept or had a beer or two. I went to sleep at once. The next thing I heard was the stewardess yelling, "Hurry! Hurry! Jump! Jump!" I opened my eyes. She was in the front of the plane jumping up and down yelling as loudly as she could and waving her arms. Believe me by this time the plane was almost empty. I took off in a hurry and jumped. I didn't think how far it was to the ground. I just jumped down the shute. When I hit the ground I hit it running like the people ahead of me. In about 60 yards they stopped as I did when I reached them. I turned around and looked—a fuel line had ruptured in the tail area not far from where I was sleeping and we could see a stream of fuel flowing down the runway. I still wonder what would have happened if this had caught on fire. They carted us back to the terminal. Those men who were having the great time were now as quiet as the rest of us. You could almost have heard a pin drop in the terminal.

When traveling by air as much as I did I saw a number of celebrities. In the late 60's my first boss, John Norton, and I were flying from Cleveland, Ohio to Buffalo, New York. At this time we flew first class. Liberace and, I assume, his agent sat across the aisle from John and me. I had the aisle seat and so did Liberace. They talked high finances all the way to Buffalo. What impressed me the most was Liberace's manner of dress. My boss was a fancy dresses but Liberace put him to shame.

I had two unusual experiences in the St. Louis Airport in the 1970s. I saw Bob Hope with three other men standing by a telephone booth. One of the men was on the phone and I walked over and said to Mr. Hope, "My Mother is a great fan of yours, would you please sign this paper for her?" He said, "Sure. What would you like me to say?" He was very nice. The man on the phone was talking with London I learned while talking to Mr. Hope. Jack Nicklaus was playing in the British Open and they were calling to find out how he was doing.

Another time I was arriving at the St. Louis Airport to meet Gene Cramer, our District Manager. I was walking from the plane to get my luggage and a man stopped me. He said, "Mr. Harvey may I have your autograph?" I told him I was not Paul Harvey. I found out later Mr. Harvey was in town and giving a talk that day. What did we have in common? Hair about the same, weight about the same, height about the same, age close. In my position I had to dress quite well. I knew I was no Paul Harvey but none the less it was a thrill to be taken for a man of his caliber.

I also got O.J. Simpson's autograph in Buffalo. We were both having dinner at the Holiday Inn Airport. He was having dinner with four other gentlemen. I assume they were football players, however I did not recognize any of them. I asked him if he would sign autographs for my two grandsons. He said, "Sure" one grandson still has his.

I have also seen lots of senators and representatives when flying out of Washington, D.C. especially on Friday evenings.

The next area I had the opportunity to open was Chattanooga, Tennessee. What a pretty area, what terrific people. I still get cards from Irene and Jim DeFrieze and Doris and Carl Barger whom I hired. We were invited to service Red Foods, the leading chain. Pruitts, the second leading chain followed. We also serviced the local independent food warehouse. We hired another woman named Mary.

I always gave my Grandfather Cole a few thoughts when traveling in Chattanooga. He lived in southern Indiana but fought on the south's side until the Battle of Lookout Mountain, just outside Chattanooga. When the south lost this battle he thought the south was going to lose and went home.

Any history buff should visit the National Park just outside Chattanooga. Fine people, fine food and great scenery.,

The next area was the Tri City area in TN. One of the prettiest areas in the United States. Harry Steffey was promoted to District Manager, Knoxville, TN. I called him Step-N-Half. His wife was very small, he called her "little Bit." I'm quite sure he still works with my grandson, Steve Butler, in the general area. I have two grandsons working for Eckrich. The other is Brad Butler in Houston, Texas.

I was asked by the company to look over the New York area. As usual, I flew in and rented a vehicle and had samples flown in. I then started out.

Homes were selling there for $100,000 to $150,000 and these were cheap but livable homes. I had seen the same homes in Findlay, Ohio, a few years back selling for $35,000. What a difference in the cost of living.

The chain buyers were very nice and up front. They liked the product and said they would authorize it. "Now what are you going to do for my company? they would say. They were selling space in the meat cases. We had never purchased space before. Once you start something like this you have to continue. The problem is, if your product doesn't move off the shelf in the allotted time you lose the space you bought.

We had a giant snow storm in New York while I was there. If you haven't driven in a snow storm in New York, you haven't driven. As a northerner, seeing southerners drive in snow in Atlanta, I thought I had seen it all. They were all over the place slipping and sliding. In New York they know how to drive in snow, but traffic was backed up for what I thought miles, bumper to bumper. I was born in Leavenworth, Indiana, the population then possibly 150, what a difference. I was impressed with the amount of our type product that was sold in the area.

I suggested we not open New York City at this time because the company would have had to change many operation directions add pay scales. I am pretty sure we are in the city now since ConAgra now owns the company.

About this time John Fitzgerald who was with Winn Dixie, Atlanta, became Meat Merchandiser of his chain in Montgomery, Albama. John had given us the opportunity to service his Georgia stores. When he was an Area Supervisor. We became, I think, good friends, at least I thought him a terrific person. Back in the 1970's, he called me 'Old Man Cole,'' John, you should see me now in 1998! I called him Big John and he was in fact big and as strong as a bull. I went to Montgomery John had me present our line to his company management team. About twenty of us sat around a huge long table. One of the men was the youngest son of the founder of Winn Dixie. He was just like all the other wealthy men I had met, common as an old shoe. John introduced me as old man Cole. John then told them why we wanted to authorize our product. I showed them the features of the product, sampled the product and sold the benefits. They agreed with John, the product had merit and should be authorized.

After the meeting John took me to see his lovely home and to meet his lovely wife. I have often wondered, after retiring, if there is as much friendship now as there was then. Honesty and friendship played a big part but of course, you had to have a good product.

While in Covington, my wife and I had quite a bit of company from Ohio especially during the winter. We called them SnowBirds. They would be on their way to Florida.

I will never forget one day my wife's niece Julene and her husband paid us a visit. We played golf all day and had several beers. When we got home Julene, said, ''I would like to ride.'' So I saddled Autumn. Autumn hadn't been ridden for awhile and I don't think a lady had ever ridden her. Pretty soon, Julene said she could not handle her. Big shot me, I said, ''I will gentle her down for you.'' I got in the saddle but did not lengthen the stirrups. About two blocks down the street a neighbor and their young Irish Setter came out. The dog ran out and nipped Autumn on the back heels. Autumn jumped sideways without warning and with nothing to brace myself with I didn't go with the horse. At that time I was in my sixties. I didn't break any bones, but the next day I was so sore I could hardly get out of bed to say goodbye to Julene and her husband.

Our next venture was Florida. We did not have to hire new people for Florida as lots of good employees were happy to transfer. Everyone wanted to go to Florida. I believe the company thought this would be fast and easy since lots of northern people spent time in Florida. It seems people from the north were in Florida to have fun not eat Eckrich lunchmeat.

The next step was Murphysboro Tennessee. Tim Sundo was appointed District Manager. I had spent some time checking independent warehouses and co-ops and they seemed to think there was room for a quality product such as Eckrich. The Company did things a little different here. We normally went into an area, leased a building that fit our needs, and as we grew we would build a new district building. Here we built a new building before starting.

CHAPTER 11

A short time later I was asked if I would accept a position of Divisional Sales Manager in Charge of the Eastern Third of the United States. This was a thrill for me and my family. Eckrich ran a story something like this, "Eckrich Revamps Their Sales Department." There were a number of promotions including my son, Brent, and myself. My hometown paper in Antwerp, Ohio, ran the story. My Mother, wanted people to know she was the Mother of Orest Cole and Grandmother of Brent Cole so she called the local newspaper advising them she was the Mother and Grandmother and they ran the story. Guess she got some calls. She was a tiger.

The president, Robert Lill, (I called him Bear) said, "It's unusual to have father and son working together. Our problem is you might work him too hard." Brent had started in sales in Findlay, Ohio, was transferred to Pittsburgh, Pennsylvania as District Manager and then became District Manager in Louisville before becoming Regional Manager.

Another extra thrill for me was when Brent and I made our first visit to the Greensburg, Indiana district and had lunch at the Greensburg Country Club. There were a number of retired Eckrich employees there among them Paul Hoffman. Paul had started the Greensburg district years ago. I called Paul "Governor" as he had been there so long. Paul had been a member of the Greensburg Country Club when they had sand greens. Man, that will date you, won't it? Al Kerect was the District Manager. These fellows lived in what I called Eckrich Village, all close together in a very nice new addition. Al was the third District

Manger that Greensburg had. Bob Stutz was the second when he retired and he was followed by Al.

Another district I visited with Brent was Brazil when Ken Ramey, who I hired years ago, was District Manager. Ken advised me Brent was a better boss than I had been. I met another man I had hired, Avery Donnley, now retired, who had helped me in a fight years and years ago.

I moved my office to Conyers, closer to Covington. I had a private secretary who had been a secretary for a company president and she helped me a great deal. I still tried to get all my people involved. From day one I felt all salespeople were competitors. I asked my Regional Managers to run weekly specials. They had each salesman report the number of ads and new authorizations they got each week. The secretary contracted each district every week and put out a weekly sales bulletin giving the details. She said she could almost see a person squirm if he or she didn't have a good report. I still did lots of traveling and was at my office only on Friday.

I spent lots of time in meetings in Fort Wayne at the corporate office. This was different work than I had ever done and I sure missed the sales contacts. I always went to see my Mother each trip to Fort Wayne, and Don Menze would let me use his car. I also attended a lot of regional meetings in the division and had at least two divisional meetings a year. Time went by in a hurry. And, suddenly, it seemed, it was time for me to leave.

There were lots of changes going on in what used to be Eckrich. Swift was now a part of the team. A number of the old gang retired or went elsewhere. Several Eckrich employees including my son Brent were transferred to Chicago. He spent three hours a day driving to and from work. He didn't like this and did not care for Chicago. Budd Lill the President, and Pat Ciez, the Marketing V.P., had left the company and were now President and VP of a meat company in Ohio. They offered Brent a position as General Sales Manager. He left Eckrich and it was the end of an era. No Coles working for Eckrich. Grandsons, yes, but their name is Butler. Beatrice Foods had purchased the

Eckrich Company and Con-Agra purchased Eckrich from Beatrice.

When I retired we were living in Georgia. My wife decided she wanted to live close to one of the children. We had one son in Northern Ohio, but she said it was too cold there. Two children lived in Florida but it was too hot in the summer. We had one daughter in Missouri and that is where we decided to move.

We had lived just outside the city limits in Covington, Georgia, and had a few acres. It was a good place for people to drop off unwanted pets. For about a week I had noticed neighbors chasing a little mixed breed dog, mostly Pekingese, off their property. One day it ran out onto the highway scared to death after all the chasing it had gone through. It seemed to know it was in dangerous territory. I stopped traffic and picked her up and took her home. I have never seen an animal so happy as she was when I picked her up. We named her Prissy. We still have her. About the same time someone dropped off a small kitten. It found our house about 2 AM. My wife heard it and brought it in the house. It is lucky to be alive because next door there were two police dogs who hated cats. How well I know, they killed our cat Hidey. We named this cat Snoopy and we still have her.

Our granddaughter Pam who lives in Kansas had a truck. She and her husband decided to bring the truck to Georgia, drop it off and go on to Florida for a vacation. When they came back we loaded the four horses into the truck and started for Missouri. About midway to Missouri the truck started overheating. We were out in the country and I was scared. I knew I couldn't fix it. My granddaughter pulled the truck over to the side of the road, raised the hood and climbed in on top of the engine. She solved the problem. I asked her how she had become such a mechanic and she told me because of her Uncle Mike.

We moved into an apartment on the east side of Columbia, Missouri and our daughter, Judy, kept the horses except for one. Pam took Misty, the filly, to Kansas City. Pam planned to show her. She showed her once and she won a blue ribbon. The filly was snake bitten and this ended ever showing her again. We found and purchased a home in Columbia. Judy was keeping the horses and Pam brought Misty home. Judy did not have enough pasture for four horses. I did not like living in the city so we purchased a place in the country with 34 acres and two ponds.

The great grandchildren enjoyed coming out to fish and ride the horses. I got a kick out of seeing our great granddaughter catch her first fish. There were some nice fish in the ponds. The kids have caught bass. I am guessing about 2 1/2 pounds, blue gills larger than your hand.

We also saddle the most gentle horse for them to ride, and who else but Autumn. Tony rides alone and Frankie who is two and a half has assistance. With his cowboy clothes, hat, shirt, pants and boots he thinks he is a genuine cowboy.

About two years ago I went back to Antwerp, Ohio, for a reunion of the 148th Infantry. Henry Donnell, now approaching 94, had served in three wars and he was my Captain. I enjoyed seeing and thanking people who helped me get a start in life. It's for sure Hank was one of those people. Hank retired from the Army a full Colonel.

While in Ohio, I visited my son Brent and his family in Sylvania, Ohio. On the way to Brent's home I stopped at Sauters Super Market to get some sheep casing franks. Bob Sauter, the owner, came over as he had recognized me after all those years. I had left the Toledo area in the 1960's. He said, ''I just wanted to tell you I enjoyed having you call on me when you were in charge at Findlay, Ohio. You never promised me a thing that you did not follow through on.'' I then visited Oscar Joseph, Jr. on my way home. They are now leasing their stories and are in the real estate business. He called his son, now grown, out of the office and said, ''I bet you don't remember this man. We used to go fishing with him.''

I stopped in and saw Don Spaulding who has since retired as a Vice President of the Food Town chain. Don was a very young man when I first called on him. These were fine people who had done a lot for me. The national chains had moved their branch offices out of Toledo so I did not get to see any of these people. I am sure all of the people I new had retired.

Youngsters who I hired are now retiring. I got a nice letter of thanks yesterday from Bob Cole (Big Time) thanking me for giving him the opportunity to work for Eckrich. Bob had a great career.

I also stopped in New Haven to see the Shaws. Both are well. They are over 80 and doing great. Evahelen was one of my teachers. Norm used to pick me up in his vehicle when I was walking to work and often advised me to get into sales.

I also saw my old boss, Don Menze. He was a Vice President of a Fort Wayne manufacturing company.

Who says friendships don't last.

During these changing times my wife was suffering from Mineirs disease. This is an incurable disease of the inner ear. It affects your balance and makes you feel as if you are spinning around all the time. She decided she wanted to live alone. We sold our house outside of Harrisburg, Missouri. My wife purchased a home in Columbia, Missouri and I moved outside Folsom, Louisiana. I took my four horses, dog and cat, and purchased a few acres. Believe me, this is quite a change for a 75 year old man.

Prissy, the dog that was dropped off in Georgia, became ill each time she had to ride in a car. She had done this for years in Georgia and in Columbia, Missouri. I asked the vet in Missouri why she did this. Her reply, "Suppose she thinks she is being dropped off again." Who said dogs are dumb?

Before leaving for Louisiana I had the car parked by the front door, loading personal things. Prissy was at the car door whining to get in. She did not become ill once on the way to Louisiana. I could not find a motel near Folsom that would accept pets so I boarded the cat, Snoopy, in Covington. I took Prissy farther south looking for a motel that would accept dogs. Prissy had a fit when I tried to leave her at the boarding place. She would not let me out of her sight. She now cries if I don't take her in the car.

On the 50th anniversary of the end of World War II, I posed with my souvenir Japanese rifle near my granddaughter Megan Butler and three of my horses.

APPENDIX

I have written this Appendix for those who like to read about wars. These are the actual conditions a person experiences during war taken from my Navy log.

Believe me, you can't describe just how frightening it is to see brave men fighting and dying. It's for sure I didn't describe how frightening it was to go alongside an ammo ship that had taken a Kamikaze hit. This is a sight you will never forget. The flack would be so thick it would seem you couldn't get through it without being killed. Through this the Skipper's voice would never crack when he was giving me orders.

I will point out a few of the most frightening experiences I went through and some of the sadest.

The most frightening was when I heard the Skipper say to the Commander, "Shall I send someone below to see if everyone has their life jackets on? I don't think we will make it." His voice was cracking. This from the bravest man I have ever known.

The sadest memories were seeing the very brave men we landed at Noemfoor standing at our fantail begging for table scraps we were throwing overboard and seeing the horrible condition they were in. Seeing all the jungle rot—the sores on there bodies—and seeing them stand on the deck leaning on their rifles, smoking cigarettes with Jap shells falling near our ship. Then watching them go down the ramp to fight and die.

My other memory is matching dog tags with the papers that listed the names of the dead; the stench of 100 bodies laying on a hot metal deck for 24 hours.

Before you begin reading the Appendix, please note these Navy terms. It has been over 50 years since I have thought of them.

LCI—Landing Craft Infantry
Battle Ship—Battle Wagon
Destroyer—Tin Can
Bow—Front end of ship
MidShip—Middle of ship
Bulkhead—Ship wall
Stern or fantail—End of ship
Cunning Tower—Where officer is stationed when ship is underway.
Pilot House—Where Quartermaster is stationed when underway.
Hatch—Door
Portside—Left side of ship
Starboard Side—Right side of ship
Hook—Anchor
Galley—Kitchen
Gangplank—A way in and out of ship.
Ladder—Steps
General Quarters—Battle stations
Head—Restroom
Red Alert—Danger-enemy near by. A sub, vessel or airplane.
Porthole—Ship window
Navy time—0001 through 2400

October 24

We were underway at 0530 smoking, 0615 ceased smoking, 0620 anchored, 0630 L.C.I. 48 moored to our starboard, 08129 G.Q., 0821 underway, 0832 started firing, 0834 ceased firing. If you wonder why the short bursts of fire—those Jap planes didn't stay long overhead when you were firing at them. 0845 started firing, 0847 ceased firing, 0850 went alongside A12 tug to assist wounded. 0912 cast off. 0952 secure G.Q., 0955 anchored 1115 G.Q., 1117 underway, 1135 started smoke, 1200 ceased smoke,

1205 started smoke, 1210 started firing, 1211 ceased firing, 1214 ceased smoking, 1229 started smoking, 1255 secured from G.Q., 1443 special sea detail underway, 1450 moored portside L.S.I. 663 for 10 drums of fog oil. L.C.I. 1065 was hit by Jap plane alongside L.S.I. 10 for more drums of fog oil and 10 smoke pots, 1707 G.Q., 1726 started smoke, 1744 started firing, 1746 ceased firing, 1752 stopped smoking, 1903 section II, 2017 condition III smoking, 2030 secure from smoking, 2045 anchored 2110 underway, 2215 anchored. These were long action filled days.

October 25

0125 underway, 0135 anchored, 0500 warmed up engines, 0505 underway, 0525 smoking, 0534 ceased smoking, 0537 alongside L.C.I. 429,0640, underway 0710 started smoke, 0722 G.Q., 0731 secure, 0848 G.Q., 0857 secured, 0945 anchored. When anchored we took our regular watches. On a small ship such as an L.C.I., the Quartermaster stands signal watch taking his turn with the signalman. When anchored, on this date and time, I was on signal watch. The Jap planes came over and they were having dogfights with our pilots. For a few seconds I just watched and enjoyed the fight. I then saw the first Kamikaze plane aim for a cargo ship just to our starboard. It just missed its bow and blew up on impact. Elmer, our mascot dog, didn't beat me to the pilot house this time as I rang G.Q., 1132d anchor secure, 1135 underway, 1136 started to smoke, 1304 started firing, 1306 gun #5 got Jap plane (Betty), 1307 ceased firing, 1436 secure from G.Q., 1557 anchored, 1625 underway red alert, 1630 started smoking, 1635 G.Q., 1642 started firing, 1643 ceased firing, 1647 started firing, 1648 ceased firing, 1735 G.Q., 1736 started firing, 1739 ceased firing, 2031 secure, 2100 steering out, men switched to hand steering, 2107 moored portside, Killies for wounded men 2125, steering fixed, underway for hospital ship, 2126 anchored longside hospital ship, 2148 cast off hospital ship.

Many times during this day Elmer, the ship's dog went up and down the ladder to and from the pilot house.

October 27

0104 anchored, 0500 underway smoking, 0616 G.Q. enemy planes, 0712 secure G.Q., 0845 G.Q., 0847 underway, 0849 started smoke, 0940 secure, 0955 anchored, 1053 underway, 1100 G.Q., 1106 started firing, 1109 ceased firing, 1110 secure G.Q., 1122 moored portside L.S.T., 1110 15 drums fog oil, 1126 underway, 1240 G.Q., 1250 started smoke, 1310 ceased smoke, 1424 anchored, 1426 secured G.Q., 1603 G.Q., 1644 secure, 1811 G.Q. enemy planes, 1820 started firing, 1822 enemy strafing us—no casualties, 1824 underway smoking, 1827 started firing, 1829 ceased firing, 1835 started firing, 1837 ceased firing, 1838 started firing, 1839 ceased firing, 1920 anchored, 2014 secured, 2031 G.Q., 2031 started engines, 2033 underway, 2035 smoking, 2105 secure G.Q., 2140 S.C.R., 2150 SCR repaired.

On October 27 about 30 P38s landed at Tacloban. The entire bay was yelling. A very happy period. Quite sure Jamor was in charge at the time. He was an ace.

October 27

0135 secured smoking, 0155 anchored engines secured, 0518 underway, 0519 started smoking, 0603 G.Q., 0630 secure smoking, 0702 secure G.Q., 0806 G.Q., 0813 secure G.Q., 0827 anchored, 1750 warmed engines, 1752 underway, 1810 anchored, 1818 G.Q., 1918 underway, 1934 smoking, 1937 secure, 1942 anchored.

October 28

0312 bomb hit nearby and blew me out of the sack. I was so tired I just got back in the sack. 0358 underway smoking, 0530 proceeding to L.C.I. 848 Tucker aboard L.C.I. with plasma, 0658 moored starboard L.C.I. 363, 0840 Tucker aboard, 0850 underway, 0910 anchored, 1130 L.C.I. 430 moored our starboard side 1604 L.C.I. 430 cast off, 1605 red alert, 1607 G.Q. enemy planes, 1610 underway, 1644 G.Q., 1650 anchored, 1754 L.C.I. 448 moored our starboard side, 1842 L.C.I. 448 underway, 1855 G.Q. underway making smoke, 1950 secure anchored.

October 29

0014 G.Q., 0055 secured, 0118 G.Q., 0132 secured, 0135 smoking, 0200 secured smoking, 0525 underway smoking, 0606 G.Q., 0649 secure, 0739 G.Q., 0147 secure, 0827 G.Q., 0832 secure, 0847 G.Q., Johns K.P. GM3/c 3293639 gun dropped index finger right hand, 0054 secure. 1215 L.C.I. 363 moored to our starboard side getting fog oil. 1325 L.C.I. 363 cast off, 1401 L.C.I. 364 moored our starboard side, 1605 L.C.I. cast off, 1838 underway, 1959 anchored, severe tropical storm shifting anchorage, 2040 underway, shifting anchorage 2112 anchored. These typhoons last about 24 hours—it takes 12 hours to reach the peak and 12 hours to recede, 2330 dragging anchor, 2355 anchored.

October 30

We shifted anchor a number of times—22 feet of cable out up to 42 feet of cable out—blacked out all this time it was very frightening. 0535 warmed engines, 0541 underway smoking, 0605 ceased smoking, 0601 red yellow alert, 0608 white yellow, 0629 anchored using bow anchor, 0632 secure engines, 0650 L.C.I. 361 moored to our starboard side, lines doubled, 1247 L.C.I. 361 cast off, 2143 L.C.>M. 472 alongside with fuel oil, 1450 L.C.M. cast off, 1532 start engines, 1538 underway, 1624 special sea detail, 1635 moored starboard side L.C.I. 361, 1700 special sea detail, 1706 cast off from L.C.I. 361, 1710 anchored, 1716 engines secured, 1816 G.Q., 1817 started firing Jap planes, 1832 secure, 2015 start engines, 2015 underway laying smoke, when do we sleep?

November 1, 1944

0317 anchored, stop smoking, 0625 L.C.I. 430 moored to portside for generator sprocket, 1248 special sea detail, 1249 started engines, 1259 L.C.I. 430 cast off. Underway after fog oil smoke, pots fog generator 40 drums, 1300 underway proceeding to AK 121 for fog oil, 1545 moored starboard side AK12, 1811 underway from AK121, 1820 anchored, 1855 start engines, 1859 underway, 2025 anchored.

November 2, 1944

0522 underway, 0743 anchored, 0748 L.C.M. 496 moored starboard side giving fuel, 0813 L.C.M. 496 cast off, 08014 L.C.I. 448 moored portside for fog drums and 24 smoke pots, 1017 underway, 1117 special sea detail, 1124 moored portside L.C.I. 28, 1245 special sea detail, started engines, 1250 underway, 1444 special sea detail, 1452 moored portside, A061 for fuel, 1643 special sea detail, started engines, 1708 underway, 1825 anchored.

November 3, 1944

0227 warm up engines, 0240 underway, 0258 plane crashed, 0456 making smoke, 0518 started firing, 0520 ceased firing, 0600 ceased smoking, 0600 enemy planes G.Q., 0641 secure from G.Q., 0650 anchored, 0655 L.C.I. 361 moored to starboard side, 0700 working party returned, 0709 received dry stores from L.C.I. 361, 0720 L.C.I. 361 received 24 smoke pots and 6 drums of fog oil from us, 0738 L.C.I. 361 cast off, 0751 L.C.I. 364 moored to our starboard side receiving 24 smoke pots and 6 fog drums, 0619 L.C.I. 364 cast off, 1036 started engines, 1050 moored portside to L.C.I. 342, 1115 received 480 rounds 20 MM ammo, 1348 special sea detail, 1351 underway, 1413 special sea detail, 1427 moored portside to Oiler 1X123, 1430 search, 1530 special sea detail, start engines, 1615 anchored, 1632 L.C.I. 363 moored to our starboard side 1714 L.C.I. 429 moored our portside, 1715 L.C.I. 363 cast off, 1800 L.C.I. 429 cast off, 2135 underway, 2145 make smoke.

November 4

0615 anchored, stopped smoking, 0838 shifting anchorage, 0850 anchored, 0900 L.C.I. 432 moored to our port, 0932 LCM moored to our starboard received 225 gallon of fuel oil, 0954 LCM 478 cast off, 1033 L.C.I. 432 cast off underway, 1122 to anchorage, 1131 anchored, 1625 L.C.I. 361 moored to our port, 1727 L.C.I. 361 cast off, 1730 underway, 2202 started smoking, 2212 ceased smoking, 2215 anchored.

November 5, 1944

0614 underway smoking, 0621 secure anchored, 14300 LCM 489 moored to our starboard side received 350 gallon fuel oil, 1432 LCM 489 cast off, 1702 LCI 448 moored to our starboard side, 1711 LCI 432 moored to our portside, 1729 LCI 448 cast off, 1736 LCI 364 moored to our starboard side, 1750 LCI 365 cast off, 1754 LCI 432 cast off, 1816 started engines, 1818 underway, 1834 anchored, 2200 underway making smoke. P.T. boat took direct hit near by enemy planes. There was nothing left except a few small pieces of board.

November 6, 1944

0540 ceased smoking, 0600 anchored, 1002 LCI 429 moored to our starboard taking our out going mail the first in about a month. 1050 LCI 429 cast off, 1740 started engines, 1745 underway proceeding to LCI 28, 1800 laying off LCI 28, 1822 special sea detail, 1830 moored starboard side LCI 361, 1839 cast off underway, 1856 anchored, 2350 underway smoking, 2400 steering out, hand steering.

November 7, 1944

0140 steering repaired, 0620 anchored, 1023 started engines, 1025 underway, 1169 special sea detail, 1122 moored portside ARL8, 1705 cast off, 1752 anchored.

November 8, 1944

0655 underway at various courses and speeds proceeding to vicinity of ARL8, 0752 anchored, 1355 dragging anchor, 1404 started engines, 1408 underway riding out storm, 1512 anchored, 1755 started engines, 1812 underway proceeding to Tacloban, 1904 anchored.

November 9, 1944

0821 work detail Tacloban. Was I surprised government had call girls for solders. Don't know how many girls. Men were lined up for I guess two blocks. Rumor was, each man was allowed three minutes. 11:45 returned LCI 447.

November 10, 1944

A very quiet day. Anchored.

November 11, 1944

0901 underway, 1029 moored starboard of the Indus for beer. The first in ages—144 cases aboard, 1114 cast off, 1125 anchored, 1129 LCI 28 moored to our starboard, 1345 started engines, dragging anchor LCI 28 cast off, 1355 underway, 1422 anchored. The following LCI moored alongside getting their beer rations from us, LCI 429 and 364 1536 underway, 1734 anchored, 1843 G.Q., 1855 secure.

November 22, 1944

0350 started engines underway, 0359 started smoking, 0610 ceased smoking, 0621 anchored, 0638 LCI 448 moored to our starboard side, 0710 started engines, 0711 LCI 448 cast off, 0717 underway, 0753 special sea detail, 0801 moored portside LCI 28, 1002 cast off underway, 1150 anchored by bow. 1355 special sea detail, 1359 underway, 1408 moored portside LCI 976, 1415 underway, 1416 G.Q., 1417 two Jap planes crashed into Achilles Liberty ship, 1418 started firing, 1418 shot down Jap Zero, 1419 ceased firing, 1451 secure G.Q., 1710 anchored, 1720 G.Q. enemy planes, 1731 started firing, 1733 ceased firing, 1750 secure, 1820 G.Q. enemy planes—five more ships hit by Kamikaze planes—what a sad sight. It seemed to the highest honor for these pilots to die, 1845 secured.

November 13, 1944

0145 started engines, 0200 underway, 0712 anchored, 0832 underway, 1040 underway for troops, 1051 beached taking aboard troops, 1103 retracted, 1117 beached more troops, 1217 retracted, 1229 anchored, 1245 started engines, 1250 underway, 1450 anchored troops aboard.

November 14, 1944

0158 started engines, 0200 underway, 0612 G.Q., 0800 beaching stations, 0804 beached, 0812 retracted, 0812 beached, 0817 troops disembarked, 0955 retracted, 1005 battle stations secured. We landed at Homonhon Island near Leyette Gulf. Part of our group landed troops at Suluan Island nearby. Don't recall any immediate firing from the soldiers. Know they were as frightened as we were. The longer you survive under these conditions the more scared you get. You see a number of ships hit by Kamikaze planes. You see a number of your sister LCI's hit the likes of LCI. 28. You have talked with a number of these people using semaphore or blinker signals. You have gone alongside ammo ships that had been hit and the ammo was exploding yet the skipper's voice never cracked. All men were frightened. If properly trained some, I think, perform better—cowards cannot. When you go alongside a ship that looks like it is exploding before your eyes you had to be scared. 1048 special sea detail, 1126 anchored, 1148 LCI 343 moored our portside, 1222 LCI 343 cast off, 1230 LCI 361 moored our portside, 1302 LCI cast off, 1810 underway, 1900 anchored.

November 15, 1944

0956 LCI 364 moored to our portside, 1006 LCI 430 moored to the starboard side, 1105 LCI 364 cast off, 1129 LCM 458 moored to our portside giving us 350 gallon fuel oil, 1150 LCI 430 cast off. We were a group flag ship with Lt. Commander Ripley aboard is why LCI's keep coming alongside for orders, 1150 LCI 436 cast off, 1347 LCI 364 moored our starboard side, 1435 LCI 364 cast off, 1442 started engines, 1451 underway, 1523 anchored, 1545 started engines, 1549 anchored, 1551 underway, 1600 special sea detail, 1612 moored starboard side LCI 972, 1627 special sea detail, 1628 underway, 1644 anchored, 1800 underway, 1830 anchored.

November 16, 1944

0713 LCI 432 moored to our portside, 0733 LCI 432 cast off, 0847 underway, 0918 beaching stations, 0945 beached White

Beach, 1015 retracted, 1132 beaching stations, 1138 beached Violet Beach, 1412 retracted these at Tacloban, 1542 special sea detail, 1551 moored longside A.O. 61 for water, 1630 cast off, 1639 moored portside LCI 363, 1654 cast off, 1708 anchored, 1748 G.Q., 1800 underway, 1818 secure G.Q., 1838 anchored.

November 17
1015 LCI 432 moored our portside taking mail, 1049 LCI 432 cast off, 1437 started engines, 1438 underway, 1452 anchored, 1530 LCI 429 moored to our starboard side, 1623 LCI 429 cast off, 1903 G.Q., 1930 secure from G.Q.

November 18, 1944
0732 G.Q., 0752 secure G.Q., 0809 G.Q., 0816 secure G.Q., 0908 LCI, 1057 moored to our starboard side, 0927 LCI 344 moored to our portside,k 0935 LCI, 1057 cast off, 1033 started engines, 1037 LCI 344 cast off, 1041 underway, 1118 anchored, 1252 started engines, 1258 underway, 1332 moored portside ARL 41, 1435 started engines, 1440 cast off, 1716 anchored.

November 19
We remained at anchor all day. Knowing the Skipper bet he had us chipping point or painting. There was no time to feel sorry for oneself.

November 20, 1944
1122 LCI 1058 moored to our portside, 1127 LCI, 1058 cast off, 1256 LCI 361 moored to our portside, 1302 LCI 361 cast off, 1505 started engines, 15222 underway, 1816 anchored San Juanico Strait 3 1/2 feet water, 25 feet cable.

November 21, 1944
1508 LCI 344 moored to our portside. 1607 LCI 344 cast off.

November 22, 1944
0828 LCI 448 moored to our portside, 1323 started engines, 1330 LCI 448 cast off, 1615 underway, 1723 anchored.

November 23, 1944

0737 started engines, 0744 underway, 0810 G.Q., 0812 secure G.Q., 0817 anchored, 0932 LCI 364 moored to our starboard side. 1302 started engines, 1304 LCI 364 cast off, 1312 underway, 1345 moored portside LCI 432, 1417 underway, 1850 G.Q., 1900 secure, 1922 anchored.

One day I saw one of our men Clarke, on deck on his knees, hands clasped. I said what are you doing? He said, "Praying for the Japs to fly over." I am from Minnesota and have done lots of hunting but shooting at these Japs is much more fun." Bet he was one in a million.

November 24, 1944

0740 G.Q., 0751 secure, 0758 G.Q., 0800 commenced firing, 0804 ceased firing, 0900 secure, 1107 G.Q., 1112 secure G.Q., 1221 LCI 347 moored to our portside, 1312 LCI 448 moored to our starboard side, 1335 LCI 448 cast off, 1345 Clarke transferred, 1456 secure, 1955 underway, 1957 started smoking, 2004 G.Q., 2050

November 25, 1944

0100 ceased smoking, 0125 anchored, 0725 LCI 432 moored to our portside, 0748 LCI 432 cast off, 0758 LCI 361 moored to our portside, 0812 LCI 363 moored to our starboard side, 0814 LCI 361 cast off, 0846 LCI 363 cast off, 0851 underway, 1008 special sea detail, 1021 we moored starboard side Indus, 1134 underway, 1250 moored starboard side LCI 363, 1416 special sea detail, 1419 underway, 1446 anchored, 1509 LCI 429 moored to our portside, 1514 LCI 344 moored to our starboard side, 1519 Higgens transferred, 1528 LCI 429 cast off, 1602 LCI 364 moored to our portside, 1607 LCI 344 cast off, 1628 LCI 432 moored to our starboard side, 1855 LCI 364 cast off, 1859 LCI 432 cast off, 2143 received orders to start smoking, 2145 started engines, 2146 start smoking, 2153 underway, 2301 stop smoking.

November 24, 1944

0012 start smoking, 0358 stop smoking, 0410 anchored, 1049 LCI 75 moored to our portside, 1059 LCI 75 cast off, 1108 LCI 171 moored to our starboard, 1108 LCI 171 cast off, 1141 G.Q., 1202 secure 1236 G.Q., 1248 secure, 1254 G.Q., 1202 secure, 1303 secure, 1329 LCI 344 moored to our portside, 1331 LCI 344 cast off, 1400 started engines, 1414 underway, 1710 anchored, 1750 LCI 343 moored to our portside, 1758 LCI 343 cast off, 1821 LCI 364 moored to our portside, 1828 LCI 361 moored our starboard side, 1829 LCI 364 cast off, 1846 LCI 361 cast off, 1857 started engines, 1900 underway, 1915 started smoking, 2030 stopped smoking, 2207 anchored.

November 27, 1944

0935 LCI 429 moored to our portside. 0950 LCI 429 cast off, 1005 LCI 430 moored to our starboard side, 1125 LCI 361 moored to our portside, 1148 G.Q., 1149 LCI 361 cast off, 1150 LCI 430 cast off, 1212 secure from G.Q., 1300 start engines, 1302 underway, 1437 anchored, 1545 underway, 1535 anchored, 1546 underway, 1611 anchored, 1620 LCI 230 moored our starboard side, 1624 Reed detached, 1625 LCI 230 cast off, 1629 underway, 1712 fire, aft, 1715 fire extinguished, 1927 anchored Kadashan Bay.

November 28, 1944

1015 LCI 1022 moored to our portside, 1102 LCI, 1022 cast off, 1309 LCI 429 moored our starboard side 1319 LCI 429 cast off, 1328 LCI 363 moored to our starboard side, 1333 LCI 363 cast off, 1739 LCI 429 moored to our starboard side, 1800 LCI 429 cast off.

November 29, 1944

0842 LCI 432 moored to our portside, 0937 LCI 364 moored starboard side, 1009 LCI 364 cast off, 1012 LCI 432 cast off, 1258 LCI 343 moored to our portside, 1317 LCI 343 cast off, 1717 LCI 343 moored to our portside, 1725 LCI 343 cast off,

1814 received orders to start smoking, condition III, 1814 started engines, 1822 underway smoking, 2118 stopped smoking, 2120 anchored, 2300 started engines, 2304 underway smoking.

November 30, 1944
0625 received orders to stop smoking, 0634 anchored, 0636 condition III, 1000 underway looking for fog oil, 1357 anchored, 2338 started smoking.

December 1, 1944
0838 started engines, 0845 underway, 0942 moored starboard side to U.S.S. Stag receiving bodies of 100 dead Americans. Navy does not bury at sea unless an absolute must. Most men in the Navy die from burns, so bodies were partly decayed when we received them. They were in canvas bags but the stench was horrible. We had these bodies aboard about 24 hours lying on a hot metal deck. We hardly had room to walk. I recall one of the crew handling an arm that had been blown off. It so decayed it just squirted out of his hands. He took off like he was shot out of a cannon. A very sad day for us. 1047 underway proceeding to the vicinity of Wasak.

December 2, 1944
Underway set course 175 degrees standard, 1739 beaching stations, 1748 beached, 1810 bodies left at beach to be handled by Army, 1815 underway retracting from beach, 2116 anchored.

December 3, 1944
0819 LCI 429 moored to our portside, 0840 LCI 429 cast off, 0921 LCI 344 moored to our starboard, 1009 Clarke aboard, 1025 LCI 230 moored to our port side, 1102 LCI 230 cast off, 1127 underway, 1556 anchored, 1626 underway, 15646 special sea detail, 1700 moored portside LCI 744, 1720 underway, 1747 anchored, 1754 LCI 432 moored to our starboard side, 2137 underway, 2148 started smoking.

December 4, 1944

0620 stop smoking, 0635 anchored, 0853 LCI 448 moored to our starboard side, 0916 LCI 448 cast off, 1039 LCI 448 moored to our starboard side, 1052 LCI 448 cast off, 1309 LCI 344 moored to our starboard side, 1336 LCI 344 cast off, 2100 underway, 2250 started to smoke, 0000 stop smoking.

December 5, 1944

0009 anchored condition III, 0400 start engines, 0412 underway, 0455 anchored, 0903 underway, 0945 moored portside LCI 448. Tokyo Rose kept sending us good music with many barbs., 1025 started engines, 1029 cast off underway, 1032 fire drill, 1032 hand steering—never a dull moment. The Skipper kept us busy., 1045 back to electric steering, 1046 fire drill secure, 1450 anchored, 1202 underway, 1243 anchored, 1335 underway, 1350 anchored—still training, 1355 anchored, 1518 started engines underway 1533. Lt. Commander Ripley aboard G. C7, 1550 commander aboard, 1600 anchored, 105 LCI 363 moored to our portside, 1647 LCI 363 cast off, 1649 LCI 430 moored our starboard side, 1835 LCI 430 cast off, 1837 LCI 429 moored to our portside, 1850 LCI 429 cast off, 2344 underway laying smoke.

December 6, 1944

0630 secure from smoking, 0636 anchored, 0748 started engines, 0754 underway, 0911 anchored, 1231 started engines, 1240 underway, 1324 beaching stations, 1351 beached Tacloban, 1332 retracted, 1342 beached, 1635 retracted practicing beaching—never a dull moment—the skipper kept us buy, 1750 moored portside LCI 432, 1830 cast off, 1842 G.Q. Jap planes sighted, 1839 secure from G.Q., 1848 anchored, 1853 started firing G.Q., 1854 ceased firing, 1869 anchored, 1905 secure G.Q.

December 7, 1944

0912 a very quite day. We were underway and anchored several times doing drills. The Skipper was a tiger but a great man in my thinking.

December 8, 1944

0901 started engines, 0912 underway, 0927 longside LCI 430 dropping off mail, 1118 anchored, 1320 LCI 343 moored our portside, 1430 LCI 343 cast off, 1711 LCI 430 moored portside, 1802 LCI 430 cast off.

December 9, 1944

0452 underway, 0618 anchored, 0653 LCI 343 moored to our starboard, 0760 LCI 343 cast off, 0745 started engines, 0750 underway, 0945 anchored in vicinity Medium 8, 1235 underway, 1255 anchored, 1500 underway, 1255 anchored, 1500 started engines, 1505 underway, 1519 special sea detail, 1523 moored starboard side to Carter Hall, 1545 cast off, 1547 special sea detail, 1722 moored portside LCI 430, 1812 cast off LCI 430, 1903 anchored.

December 10 and 11 not exciting; we just kept training, chipping paint, upgrading charts, etc.

December 12, 1944

0856 started engines, 0905 underway, 0931 special sea detail, 0940 moored starboard side Hughes DD 420 to pick up bodies, 1320 started engines, 1325 underway, 1702 FA 47-2 EA 45 longside to remove deceased, 1714 deceased all removed, 1845 special sea detail, 1850 moored portside to LCI 343, 1914 underway to anchor, 1922 anchored.

December 13, 1944

0525 engines started, 0615 underway making smoke broke down smoking, 0655 anchored, 1052 LCI 448 moored to starboard side, 1058 LCI 448 cast off, 1333 LCI 429 moored to starboard side, 1438 LCI 429 cast off, 1805 engines repaired.

December 14, 1944

0805 started engines, 0810 underway, 0931 anchored, 1051 started engines, 1058 underway, 1112 moored portside to 65S

Haraden DD 585, 1122 G.Q., 2238 secure G.Q. We were along-side to pick up bodies. This is sure a sad experience. 1217 cast off underway for Tacloban, 1709 beached, 1801 deceased ashore, retracted from beach, 1812 underway to anchorage, 2015 anchored.

December 15, 1944

0806 LCI 363 moored to our portside, 0826 LCI 363 cast off, 0849 LCI 331 moored to our starboard side, 0845 LCI 331 cast off, 0859 LC131 moored to our portside, 0913 LCI 131 cast off, 1310 underway, 1354 moored starboard side HSS Stag for water, 1520 underway, 1617 moored portside LCI 432, 1631 cast off underway, 1645 moored portside LCI 363, 1744 underway, 1752 anchored.

December 16, 1944

0800 chipping paint, painting and correcting charts, 1558 started engines, 1603 underway proceeding to LCI 361 for meat (Mutton) and vegetables. Mutton was terrible but much better than KC rations. 1620 moored portside LCI 361, 1639 supplies aboard, 1724 underway, 1934 anchored.

December 17, 1944

0933 LCI 343 moored to our portside, 1053 LCI 343 cast off. Throughout the day these LCI's were longside receiving orders LCI 430, 448 and 432.

December 18, 1944

0700 started engines, 0710 secured engines, 1243 start engines. 1245 underway, 1300 moored portside LCI 448, 1412 cast off, underway, 1536 special sea detail, 1548 moored starboard side LST 909, 1614 troops aboard, 1616 cast off, set true course 115 degrees, 1828 beaching stations, 1847 beached—no enemy fire at us, happy day. Am sure the troops we landed were frightened as we were when we landed them. 1900 retracted from beach., 1905 secure beaching stations. 2205 anchored.

December 19

0803 started engines, 0800 underway, 0934 anchored, 1052 LCI 228 moored to our portside, 1104 LCI 228 cast off. We had 20 men aboard this day transferring them from one small island to another. They were part of the 225 field artillery, 2945 anchored.

December 20

0810 underway, 0825 moored portside LCI 432, 0911 started engines, 0913 underway, 0952 moored starboard side USS Louisville 28, 1002 cast off underway, 1022 special sea detail, 1040 moored starboard side Phoenix, 1106 cast off, 1210 special sea detail, 1226 moored portside Liberty Ship John Evans, 1346 cast off, underway, 1402 anchored 1419 SC 729 moored to our starboard side, 1500 SC729 cast off, 1528 underway, 1649 moored portside Phoenix 1723 underway, 1751 moored portside the Louisville 1825 cast off, 1851 GQ. 1905 secure, 1909 anchored, 1920 received orders to start smoking condition III, 2015 secure smoking, 2135 anchored, 2138 to 2328 repair fog generator December 21 to December 24. Nothing exciting—drills, chipping paint, painting, a few off limits poker and crap games.

December 25, 1944

This sure as hell was not home. Among other things the Skipper was a minister. We had church services as we did every Sunday, although he did not force us to attend. The Japs didn't know it was Christmas. At 2130 we were underway smoking until 2216 we ceased smoking and anchored. Our cook, Whiskey Joe, prepared Christmas dinner.

December 26

0628 LCI 430 anchored to our portside, 0725 LCI 430 cast off. Throughout the day LCI 362, 344, 448, and 449 kept mooring alongside meeting with Lt. Commander Ripley. Think we were quitting around Leyte Gulf.

December 27, 1944 Anchored

December 28, 1944
We had condition III and smoked from 1930 until 2006.

December 29
0415 started to smoke, 0427 anchored, 0745 smoke generator broke and was repaired.

December 30, 1944
0207 condition II started to smoke generator inoperative. Think this equipment like the crew was exhausted. 1030 generator repaired.

January 1, 1945
Smoke generator had been repaired. It seems now at night is when we have condition III, 2130 underway to smoke, 2240 ceased smoking, 2334 smoking, 2350 smoke generator again broke, 2359 anchored.

January 2, 1945
0745 smoke generator repaired.

January 3, 1945
Underway smoking 2333

January 4, 1945
0545 ceased smoking, 0600 anchored.

January 6
Smith Nick A5 1/C received lacerations on little finger, left hand. PHM 1/C Tucker promptly took care of this. Tucker had kept us

all healthy for months. 1340 LT. JG A.F. McCormick detached. Anchored.

January 7 Anchored all day.

January 8, 1945
1012 fire aft, 1015 fire out. Anchored all day.

January 9
Church party aboard, 1102 anchored by stern expecting storm—no storm.

January 9 through 12 —Training.

January 13, 1945
0753 started engines underway from Dulag for Tolasa, 0837 beaching stations, 0842 beached Tolasa. We picked up General Mudge and his aides transporting them to APA47 moored starboard side General and his aides aboard APA47, 1700 cast off, 1703 anchored, 1712 just off Tolsas.

January 14, 1945 Training while anchored.

January 15, 1945
0625 underway, 0659 beaching stations, 0705 beached Tolasa, 0710 General Mudge and his aides aboard, 0715 secure beaching, 1047 working party aboard APA47, 1130 General Mudge and party again aboard, 1346 beaching stations, 1351 beached Tolasa, 1345 General and party ashore, 1403 retracted from beach, 1412 anchored.

January 16, 1945
1012 still training fire drill aft, 1015 hand steering. The Skipper kept us busy all the time.

January 1, 18, 19 Training while anchored.

January 20, 1945

1330 LCI 363 moored alongside our starboard side. 1348 supplies from LCI 363 fresh cabbage. The first fresh vegetables in months. Whiskey Joe will fix us a feast. Mutton from New Zealand.

January 21 through 25 Training. Anchored all day.

January 26, 1945

underway 0754 drills all day—fire, hand steering G.Q. abandon ship, beaching Tanauan twice secured and anchored 1750.

January 27, 1945

0732 underway, 0855 beaching stations, 1010 retracted 1021 beached, 1038 troops aboard, 1117 retracted, 1150 anchored, 1200 G.Q., 1215 secure G.Q.

January 28, 29, 30 Underway with troops.

January 31, 1945

1020 beaching stations, 1027 beached, 1034 troops ashore, 1036 retracted, 1059 secure beaching stations, 1450 base course 179, 1621 Heffner Kenneth V. suffered sulfuric acid burns. PhM 1 C Tucker to the resure. Doc as Tucker is known made him a new man. We are now on Luzon, Japan getting closer. We hear less of Tokyo Rose, 1910 anchored.

February 1, 1945

0800 we are moving fast now, 1033 underway, 1128 anchored, 1235 start engines, 1239 underway, 1337 anchored, 1330 LCI 344 moored to our portside.

February 2, 1945

0220 Received 5,000 gallons of fuel oil from LCI 344, 1043 started engines, 1202 lying off LCI 972, 1228 anchored, 1245 LCI 430 moored our starboard side, 1330 LCI 430 cast off, 1337 dragging anchor, 1345 underway, 1352 beaching station, 1407 beached Mindoro, 1620 beaching stations, 1630 retracted from beach, 1710 beaching stations, 1725 beached, 1345 started engines.

February 3, 1945
0004 retracted, 0124 anchored, 0644 started engines, 0650 underway, 0713 moored starboard side LCI 978, 0745 started engines, 0747 cast off. Underway to anchorage, 0945 anchored, 1012 LCI 430 moored our starboard side, 1349 LCI 430 cast off, 1356 beaching stations, 1406 beached, 1500 retracted, 1509 underway, 1644 anchored.

February 4, 1945
0014 started engines, 0017 underway, 0115 beaching stations, 0124 beached, 0145 retracted, 0220 anchored, 1745 start engines, 1750 underway, 1812 beaching stations, 1822 beached, 1824 secure.

February 5, 1945
0200 started engines, 0215 retracted, 0228 anchored with bow, 0232 secure, 1053 LCI 430 moored to our starboard side, 1318 LCI 430 cast off, 1319 started engines, 1328 underway, 1338 beaching stations, 1345 beached, 1337 secure, 1422 anchored. We were sure doing lots of maneuvering and drawing no fire. We knew the Japs had not given up—Tokyo Rose told us so.

February 6, 1945
1020 started engines, 1023 underway, 1030 beaching stations, 1043 retracted underway, 1054 special sea detail, 1104 moored portside LCI 972, 114 special sea detail, 1116 underway, 1152 beaching stations, 1200 beached, 1201 secure.

February 7, 1945
1132 started engines, 1206 secure engines, 1403 started engines, 1429 retracted from beach, 1433 underway, 1450 special sea detail, 1518 moored portside LCI 960, 1529 secure, 1606 started

engines, 1612 underway to beach, 1618 beaching stations, 1622 beached, 1625 secure, 2230 Bagarella stomach cramps. As usual PHM 1/C W. F. Tucker was there and he was given 1/2 gm morphine. Cramps returned 2400 and was given 1 1/2 gr morphine and sodium penathal.

February 8, 1945

Tucker did it again—Bagarella was fine. Tucker felt Bagarella had been drinking to much of Whiskey Joe's home made booze. 1315 started engines, 1400 retracted, 1410 underway proceeding to vicinity of AD 26 and K54, 1545 anchored vicinity of K54, 1656 LCI 970 moored our starboard side, 1709 LCI 970 cast off.

February 9, 1945

0345 LCI 747 moored to our starboard side, 0345 LCI 577 moored to our portside, 0747 LCI 747 cast off, 0912 LCI 577 cast off, 0945 started engines, 0956 underway, 0618 special sea detail moored starboard LCI 747, 1037 cast off, 1041 anchored, 1051 LCI 1015 moored to our starboard side, 1115 LCI 661 moored to our portside, 1125 LCI 1015 cast off, 12112 LCI 661 cast off, 1415 started engines, 1425 underway, 0425 special sea detail, 1445 moored portside LCI 430, 1630 started engines, 1645 underway, 1700 moored starboard side LCI 747, 1713 underway proceeding to LCI 661, 1720 moored portside LCI 661, 1730 cast off underway, 1830 beaching stations, 1839 beached, 1845 secure.

February 10, 1945

0800 started engines, 0808 beaching stations, 0812 retracted underway, 0915 anchored, 1300 started engines, 1315 secured engines, 1830 started engines, 1836 underway, 1842 beaching station, 1846 retracted, 1848 underway to X125, 1920 special sea detail, 2042 moored portside to X125, 2044 secure, 2100 LCI 430 moored to our starboard side, 2305 started engines, 2315 LCI 430 cast off, 2318 underway, 2325 anchored by stern.

February 11, 1945

0915 started engines, 0928 underway, 0929 beaching stations, 0939 beached, 0940 secure. With all these beaching we knew something big was coming up. We were scared but I think we wanted to be involved. We knew Japan had to be whipped before we could return home. The longer we were involved in fighting seeing the dying and wounded the more frayed our nerves got. At this point we had been very fortunate. We were strafed once by Jap planes and had one person who had a nervous breakdown. Quite sure he was an atheist. In my thinking you had better believe in the man upstairs. When I left for the war my Catholic neighbors gave me a St. Christopher medal. When things were tough, I'd guess I rubbed this medal a couple of dozen times a day.

We had a fine crew in my thinking. The officers SW Goldsmith, Skipper T. C. Tatgenhorst, W. B. Schlosser, A. J. McCormick and J. D. McDade had a lot to do with this. The Skipper was fair but strict. He had a few captain's mast, nothing serious, sleeping etc. Sleeping on watch could have been serious but in this case it wasn't. Don't think I ever saw a fight among us. It's amazing how people reacted under battle conditions. All were scared, but if well trained and with good leadership all could preform; only a few would be so nervous they would throw up. Others who could recognize Jap planes in less than a second on film couldn't recognize them in a number of seconds when the planes were coming towards us. When we were beached we played a little touch football.

You couldn't believe how suntanned we were. Except when standing watch all we wore was a pair of shorts and a pair of heavy wooden soled sandals. Sandals had to be thick soled because of the metal deck. In the afternoon the deck was so hot you could almost fry an egg on it. The hot deck was another reason the dead bodies deteriorated so rapidly.

February 12 through 15 Training.

On **February 15** a picture appeared in the Pittsburgh Sun Telegraph of the LCI 447 hitting the beach with troops.

February 16, 1945
1410 started engines, 1413 beaching stations, 1440 retracted, 1455 beached, 1452 secure.

February 17, 1945
Started engines, 1500 secured engines.

February 18 and 19—beached as before.

February 20, 21 beached as before. Received 7,000 gallons water from beach. 2158 LCI 977 moored to our portside.

February 22, 1945
0657 started engines, 0728 special sea detail, 0805 LCI 977 cast off, 0806 retracted from beach, 0816 beaching stations, 0832 beached. Major transferred.

February 23, 1945
0040 start engines, 0045 retracted, 0050 anchored, 0620 started engines, 0634 underway, 1327 LCI 1021 in tow, 1750 G.Q. drill, 1752 started firing, 1753 ceased firing, 1758 secure G.Q.

February 24, 1945
0035 LCI 1021 cast off, 0055 anchored, 0750 started engines, 0804 underway, 0920 special sea detail, 0925 moored portside LCI 774, 0930 secure, 0940 cast off, 0950 anchored, 1007 LCI 430 moored to our starboard, 1015 started engines, 1016 LCI 430 cast off, 1019 underway, 1228 anchored, 1501 started engines, dragging anchor, 1612 underway, 1716 anchored by stern, 1718 secure, 1821 LCI 343 moored to our portside, 1840 LCI 343 cast off, 1852 LCI 448 moored to starboard side. 1920 LCI 448 cast off.

February 25 we were training-beaching retracting through **February 28** Never a dull moment.

March 1, 1945
0215 underway searching for ARL 40, 0922 moored starboard side to ARL 40, 1132 cast off, 1328 special sea detail, 1335 moored starboard side USS Remus, 1339 cast off, 1412 anchored.

March 2 through March 20 more and more training. Example, on March 15 at 1325 started engines, 1336 LCI 344 moored to our portside, 1340 LCI 344 cast off, 1345 underway to Tacloban, 1426 G.Q., 1435 secure G.Q., 1436 fire aft, 1437 hand steering, 1439 electric steering, 1441 all secure, 1748 anchored by stern, 1751 secure.

March 16 through March 10 more of the same—we were kept busy.

March 21, 1945
1458 started engines, 1510 underway, 1626 anchored near beach, 1825 started engines, 1831 beaching stations, 1842 beached, 1849 retracted, 1900 beached, 1901 beaching secure, 1920 LCI 448 moored to our portside, 2000 LCI 448 castoff, 2221 troops aboard, 2241 special sea detail, 2258 anchored.

March 22, 1945
0550 started engines, 0653 underway. We varied our course eleven times beaching at 1743 beaching at Ormoc, Leyte other side of island from Tacloban. We had 250 men aboard from Company Mand H0 40th Division. We had no ground fire. I have such names as this in my log book which I can't locate on the maps I have but I am quite sure they are in the vicinity of Ormoc, Cape Blanco, Brunco, Port Palampa and Oetorara.

With this leisure time we had a few more Captain's Mast. During this time we had been up and down the coast of Luzon Subie Bay Clark Field Lingayen Gulf. I sure enjoyed talking with the fighter pilots around Clark Field. In their minds they were the best and they proved it over and over again. In my opinion, if it hadn't been for the Kamikaze planes the war would have been over by this time. If the Kamikaze wasn't shot down by ship or airplanes they seldom missed. The longer you saw this suffering and horrible death the more you wondered, will I be next. They were not after a small ship such as an LCI but when they were hit they would take anything in sight.

While in Luzon we had our first liberty—it was the first for me in sixteen months and for the original crew 22 months. Port and starboard each had twelve hours. When starboard failed to show port took off. I was on portside. There wasn't much to see—bamboo huts with people sleeping on mats. Jap rice whiskey was available as well as sake (Jap wine). Both were better than the Tumba juice available at Tacloban. The town we visited was Cavite just about six miles from Manilla. We could see the lights but I didn't think anyone went there, as it would have been along walk. People didn't seem that happy to see us in their town. The pictures I have seen on television seem to show the people have not upgraded themselves very much. But maybe they only show the bad pictures on television.

There is only one place I would like to visit in this world and that's New Guinea. I would like to see if they upgraded themselves as it is for sure it couldn't be worse.

At 1906 we retracted from beach, 1914 anchored.

March 23, 1945
0940 underway, 1300 anchored, 1312 underway to Tacloban, 1358 fire drill, 1408 fire drill secure, 1408 G.Q., 1418 secured G.Q., 1425 small arms practice. All these months had a sub machine gun in the pilot house and on this day I shot 10 rounds at tin cans. What do you know I missed. I wasn't as good a shot as Clarke. 1844 anchored in strait.

March 24, 1945
0624 we knew something big was coming up and we were not going to be involved. This was the first island hop since Noemfoor that we hadn't been involved in. We were happy and yet

sad. We knew there was more fighting to do before we got to to home.

March 25 through March 31
we kept busy training, chipping paint, painting and fixing charts.

April 1—April Fools Day. The invasion of Okinana. It almost seemed as if we were there, firing at those many Kamikaze planes.

April 1 through April 11 Training.

April 12 through April 23 when my log book ran out, we just kept training, a couple liberty parties at Smar, taking on fuel and water and Australian mutton.

My log book ran out. I could not take the one that was being used.

Sometime after April 23 we heard we were going south and we felt sure it was Australia and liberty. We had liberty but it was in New Guinea. Humbolt Bay with liberty in Hollanda. We were sent there for new engines for the invasion of Japan.

A Quartermaster stands signal watch on a small ship. When anchored I stood watch four hours and was off eight hours. I upgraded the maps and practiced signal light and semaphore with Roy Vetter. He was better than I of course. His rate was Signalman. Roy could read a light as fast as anyone could send. He just held the light open. By this time I was a Second Class Quartermaster. Mr. Tag couldn't understand why I wasn't studying for First Class. I knew with a good a job with an excellent company and waiting for me a wife and two children. I wasn't going to make the Navy a career.

First Class Quartermaster has to be quite knowledgeable shooting the stars, plotting courses and etc. Mr. Tag wanted everyone to be the best he could be. The training I received from

Mr. Tag and Mr. Goldsmith served me well in later life. Both were brave and high on integrity.

The other officers were also but my job did not bring me into contact with them.

I happened to be on signal watch on June 6 when everyone started to put up flags—they read victory. I didn't think the Japs would surrender this easily. The war in Europe was over. Mr. Tag detached and headed for duty in U.S. He took uncensored letters with him from all of us.

We continued to drill and play touch football waiting for the new engines.

The battle was still raging on Okinawa early June. We heard on June 19, 1945 the Japs were surrendering by the hundreds and dying by the thousands. Rumor had it the Japs had flown 1900 suicide missions, many more than we had seen in the Philippines.

On August 6th we heard a powerful new type bomb had been dropped by a B29.

One the morning of August 15 I was on signal watch when again the victory flags were run up. I tell you the LCI 447 was not the last ship in the harbor to run up the victory flag. We had a half month's beer ration aboard and didn't wait for it to get cold—we drank it warm. We all wanted to get home. I had my points in and being married with children with a job to go to I was, I think, the first one transferred to the island for transportation home. We were assembled there for a week waiting for transportation. It seemed like years.

I was then homeward bound—WAR OVER!